PRACTICAL STATISTICAL METHODS FOR QUALITY IMPROVING PRODUCTS, SERVICES, AND PROCESSES

A guide to statistics using Minitab® Statistical Software with step-by-step instructions and data sets

Matthew A. Barsalou

Quality in Education Think Tank (QiETT)
INTERNATIONAL ACADEMY FOR QUALITY

© **Matthew Barsalou 2021**

Published by the International Academy for Quality's Quality in Education Think Tank (QIETT)

MINITAB® and all other trademarks and logos for the Company's products and services are the exclusive property of Minitab Inc. All other marks referenced remain the property of their respective owners. See minitab.com for more information.

Although the author and publisher have made every effort to ensure that the information in this book was correct at press time, the author and publisher do not assume and herby disclaim any liability to any party for any loss, damage, or disruption caused by error so omissions, whether such errors or omissions result from negligence, accident, or any other cause.

Dedications

This book is dedicated to Michael Buckner, Sandra Dreja, Marco Fernschield, Vanessa Friese, Christina Gronowski, Thomas Leger, and Dimitri Schamrin

Table of Contents

ACKNOWLEDGEMENT 2
PREFACE 2
INTRODUCTION 2
CHAPTER 1: INTRODUCTION TO MINITAB AND STATISTICS 2
CHAPTER 2: EXPLORING DATA GRAPHICALLY 2
CHAPTER 3: HYPOTHESIS TESTING 2
CHAPTER 4: REGRESSION ANALYSIS 2
CHAPTER 5: CAPABILITY STUDIES 2
CHAPTER 6: STATISTICAL PROCESS CONTROL 2
CHAPTER 7: DESIGN OF EXPERIMENTS 2
CHAPTER 8: CONCLUSION 2
APPENDIX A: BUILD A DIY CATAPULT FOR DESIGN OF EXPERIMENTS 2
APPENDIX B: BUILD A PAPER HELICOPTER FOR DESIGN OF EXPERIMENTS 2
APPENDIX C: GENERATING RANDOM DATA IN MINITAB 2
REFERENCES 2

Acknowledgement

I would like to thank Eston Martz, my former editor at the Minitab Blog, who many years ago published my first writing.

I would also like to thank Vanessa Friese (Instagram Portfolio: @vanessarottencandy) for providing many of the illustrations in the section "Flight of the Chickens,"Dr. Kamran Moosa of the PIQC Institute of Quality for helping in preparing the manuscript for publication, and Dr. Pedro Manuel Saraiva of the University of Coimbra for making this work accessible to those who need it through the QiETT.

Preface

The section called "Keep your Redshirt on: A Bayesian Exploration" was originally published at

www.significancemagazine.com

and "If you Don't Understand your Statistics, they can Become a Liability" was published by *StatsLife*. Much of the meaning material was originally published by the *Minitab Blog*. What all of the sections have in common is that they were written to communicate basic statistical concepts in an easy to understand way.

Statistics is a serious subject, but that does not mean it always needs to be presented in a dry and technical way. This material was writing using simple, and occasionally ridicules, examples so that people of various backgrounds can follow them and apply the concepts. This material is intended to teach statistical methods using Minitab Statistical Software and if you occasionally find reason to laugh while doing so, then even better.

The data sets used can be found at the following link if you would like to follow along in Minitab:

https://drive.google.com/file/d/1y6iQPJrUpVe-PvNbF78Ih-eIMRyghnxI/view?usp=sharing

Introduction

Chapter one introduces both Minitab[R] Statistical Software and statistics. Basic concepts and the history of statistics are also explained. Charter two explains Exploratory Data Analysis and the use of graphs. Chapter three presents hypothesis testing and chapter four explains how to perform a regression analysis.

The fifth chapter describes how to perform a capability study and the seventh chapter introduces Statistical Process Control. The next covers Design of Experiments and the final chapter is the conclusion.

There are three appendixes. The first one explains how to build a catapult for Design of Experiments and the next one explains how to construct a paper helicopter. The final appendix explains how to create random data in Minitab for practicing statistical methods using Minitab.

CHAPTER 1

Introduction to Minitab and Statistics

This chapter describes the use of statistics as well as a providing a brief history of the field. People often make jokes when I tell them of my interest in statistics; these people may be failing to appreciate the seriousness of statistics. An improperly performed study or misinterpreted result could result in a financial loss when defective parts are produced or even loss of life if a dangerous medicine is brought on the market.

Statistical practitioners should understand statistical methods and where these methods came from. There are also statistical methods used primarily in industry; these include Statistical Process Control and Response Surface Methodology. An overview of the many options in Minitab is also provided in this chapter.

An improperly defined variable of interest or a poorly executed study could lead to the wrong conclusion. Therefore, forming an operational definition to properly describe the variable of interest is also presented as well as commentary on proper data collection for carrying out a statistical study.

1.1   Statistics: No Laughing Matter

I told a friend about my interest in statistics, and he immediately told me a joke about broiled chicken and statistics.

The punch line involved my friend getting to eat all the chicken. Unfortunately, I forgot the rest of the joke. I can, however, assure you it was a very funny statistics-related joke.

People often make jokes when I mention my interest in statistics, and I don't think they make the jokes just because there are so many great statistics-related jokes available. There might be some good jokes about statistics, but I only know two and can only remember one.

I also don't think people make jokes about statistics because it is an inherently hilarious subject. It can be an *interesting* subject, but it is seldom a *funny* subject.

In fact, the subject can be deadly serious. In public health, statistics can be used to identify cancer clusters and to validate the effectiveness of medical test (Greenhalgh 1997). Failing to identify a cancer cluster or the presence of a disease or disorder in an individual could result in a medical problem going untreated.

There is also the opposite risk—falsely identifying a cancer cluster in a community or a disease in an individual. This would mean resources are wasted on healthy people, as well as the negative consequences which could result when a healthy person is given an incorrect terminal diagnosis. Being falsely diagnosed with terminal cancer is more than just statistics; it is a life-changing, personal tragedy for the person who was misdiagnosed (Holt 2013).

For those of us using statistics in manufacturing, the consequences of improper use of statistics may not be as severe as in the medical field. It is still a serious subject. An improperly performed or simply flawed study could result in a product that angers formerly loyal customers, as the Coca-Cola Company learned when they introduced New Coke in 1985 (Coca-Cola Company 2012). The correct use of statistics can have series consequences for the safety of consumers and a company's financial well-being if a statistical study fails to identify a serious hazard in a product. There can also be financial consequences if a study incorrectly identifies a safety hazard where none exists.

Statistics are used in medical testing to determine both whether or not potential new medicines work, and to determine if they have unwanted side effects. Statistics are also used to determine if the benefits of some medicines outweigh the risks of using them. Here, an incorrect interpretation of statistical data could result in harming people with medicine that that was intended to help them.

The consequences of making a mistake when using statistics in business are not always severe; however, they could be. An improperly analyzed Student's t-test may result in an implementing an expensive improvement that actually does not change anything about the product. Or it could result in the product unknowingly becoming less safe than it was before the improvement was implemented.

We may not even realize when the consequences of a statistical mistake could be severe.

For those of us who use statistics, but are not trained statisticians, fortunately there are resources available to help us in correctly selecting and applying statistical methods. The National Institute of Standards and Technology collaborated with the semiconductor industry's SEMATECH to produce a free online statistics handbook (NIST/SEMATECH 2017). Statistical practitioners can also attend training by universities, professional societies and industry. Practitioners can also attend training offered by Minitab.

To make up for the seriousness of this subject—as well as my inability to remember the statistics joke, I mentioned at the start—I'll finish with this classic statistics joke:

> *Three statisticians went duck hunting. A duck flew out and the first statistician took a shot, the shot went a foot too high. The second statistician took his shot and the shot went a foot too low. The third statistician said, "We got it!"*

1.2 A Brief Illustrated History of Statistics for Industry

The field of statistics has a long history and many people have made contributions over the years. Many contributors to the field were educated as statisticians, such as Karl Pearson and his son Egon Pearson. Others were people with problems that needed solving, and they developed statistical methods to solve these problems.

The Standard Normal Distribution One example is Karl Gauss and the standard normal distribution, which is a key element in statistics. The distribution was used by Gauss to analyze astronomical data in the early nineteenth century and is also known as the Gaussian distribution or more simply, the bell curve.

Any normal distribution can easily be converted into the standard normal distribution based on a Z score table. The standard normal distribution is often used when comparing the means of either large samples or populations. For example, an engineer may perform hypothesis testing using the standard normal distribution to compare before-and-after results when attempting to increase the mean of a manufacturing process.

Student's t Distribution The well-known Student's t distribution was created by a Guinness brewery employee named William Sealy Gosset, who published in the journal *Biometrika* under the name Student (Student 1908). Guinness did not permit its employees to publish because of fear of the competition learning about what they were doing, hence Gosset published under a pseudonym (Salsburg 2001).

Gosset created Student's t distribution because previous formulas for estimating the error of samples required a large sample size and Gosset had found that there were often only small samples available. Student's t distribution is used for small sample sizes and approaches the standard normal distribution as sample size increases (see Fig. 1.1).

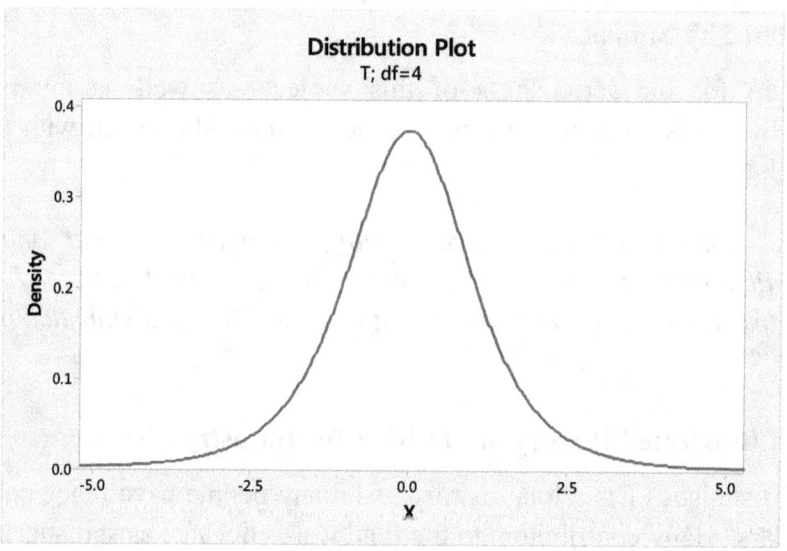

Figure 1.1: t distribution

This aspect permitted Gosset to perform experiments with small sample sizes, and this distribution is just as useful in industry today as it was when Gosset created it. For example, small sample sizes are more economical if a manufacturer wanted to perform experiments on expensive products and the experiments required destructive testing.

Shewhart and Control Charts In 1924, Walter A. Shewhart presented the management of Western Electric's Hawthorne plant with his concept of Statistical Process Control (SPC). In his 1931 book *Economic Control of Quality of Manufactured Product,* Shewhart explained that eliminating assignable causes of variation would lead to a reduced level of inspection and therefore both higher quality and lower costs (1980).

Using control charts such as an Xbar-R chart, a manufacturer can quickly tell when a process is at risk of producing defective parts without needing to individually inspect every item after production. Control charts can also detect a problem before hundreds or thousands of defective parts have been produced (see Fig. 1.2).

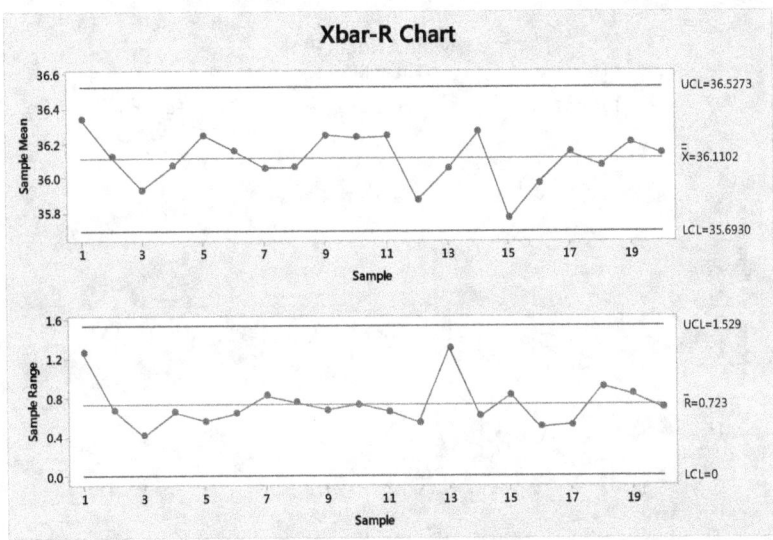

Figure 1.2: Xbar-R chart

Design of Experiments Four years after Shewhart published *Economic Control of Quality of Manufactured Product*, Ronald A. Fisher published his classic work *The Design of Experiments*. Fisher explained the proper methodology for performing Design of Experiments (DoE) (1971).

Today, DoE is frequently used in industry for performing experiments and is a key part of the Six Sigma quality improvement methodology. One of the great advantages of DoE is the ability to reduce the number of experimental runs required to get usable results. An experiment performed using DoE can provide the experimenter with information on the main effects of varying the levels of the experimental factors, as well as the interactions between the factors when the levels are varied (see Fig. 1.3 and Fig. 1.4).

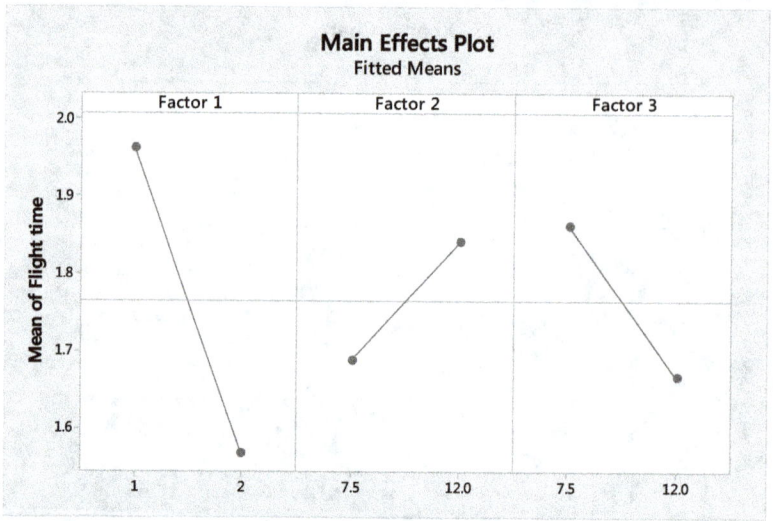

Figure 1.3: Main effects plot

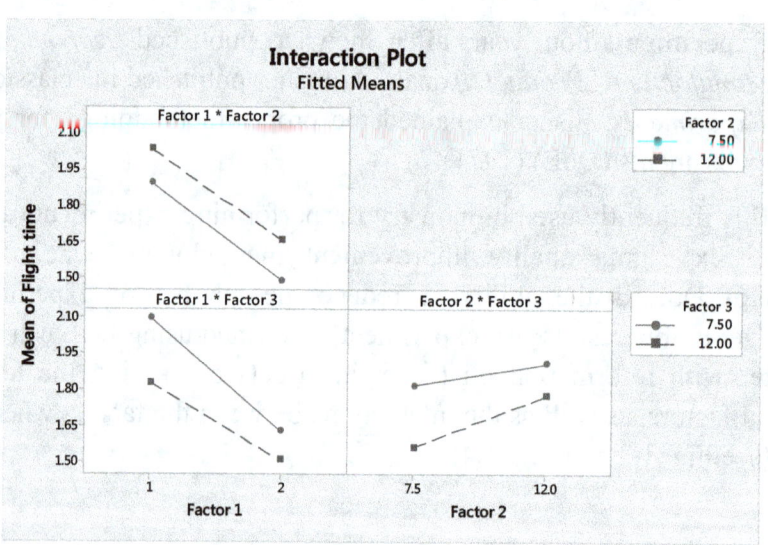

Figure 1.4: Interaction plot

Fisher's future son-in-law George E. P. Box, with K. B. Wilson, further advanced DoE. They introduced the concept of Response Surface Methodology (RSM) in 1951 (1951). This variation on DoE is used to determine the relationship between multiple factors and one or more output variables in order to determine an optimal response. It can be used for process improvement, troubleshooting, and for making a product more robust to outside influences. Response surface methods can be used to produce both surface and contour plots for analyzing the effects of varying influence factors on a product or process (see Fig. 1.5 and Fig. 1.6).

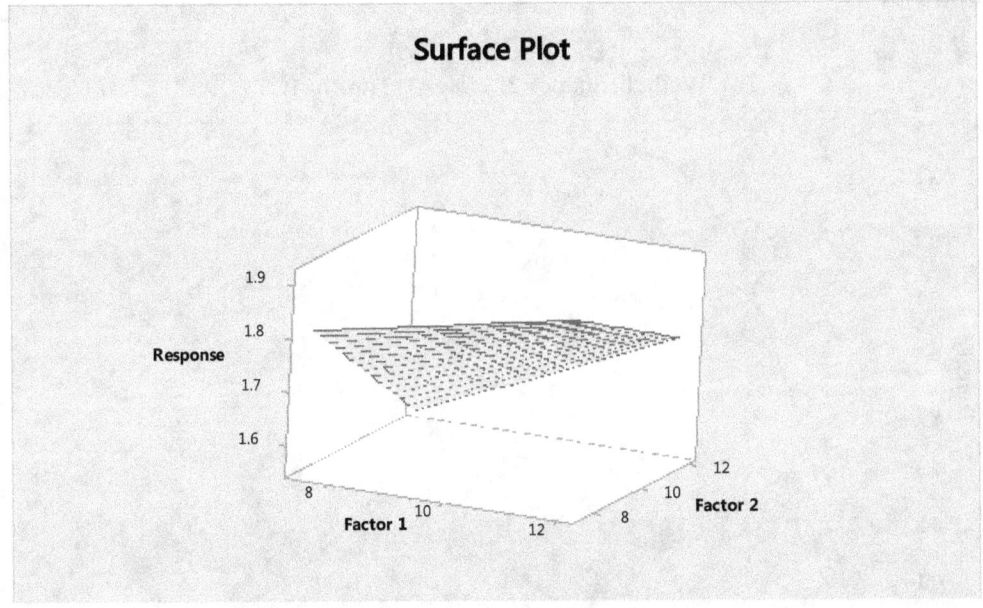

Figure 1.5: Surface plot

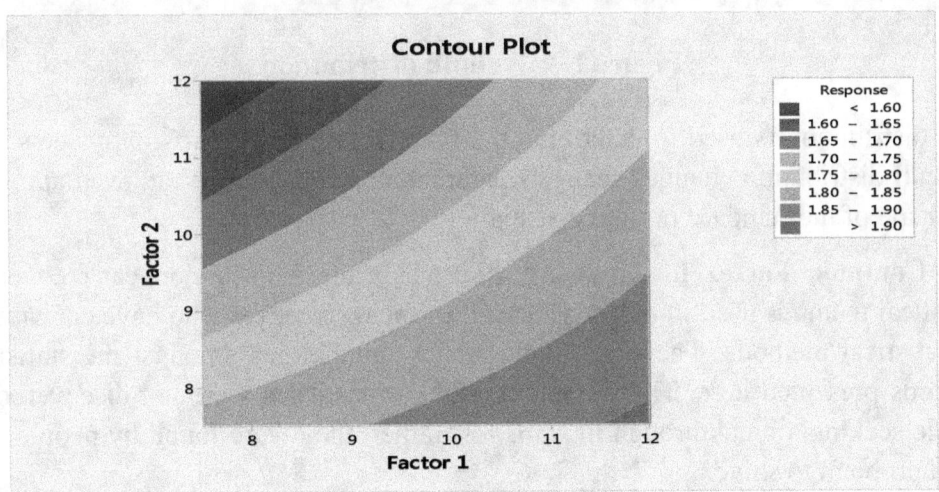

Figure 1.6: Contour plot

The Weibull Distribution The Weibull distribution is named for E. H. Waloddi Weibull and is frequently used in the field of reliability engineering. Weibull was not the first to discover the distribution that bears his name; however, he brought the Weibull distribution to prominence when he introduced in to the American Society of Mechanical Engineers (ASME) in 1951 (see Fig. 1.7) (O'connor and Kleyner).

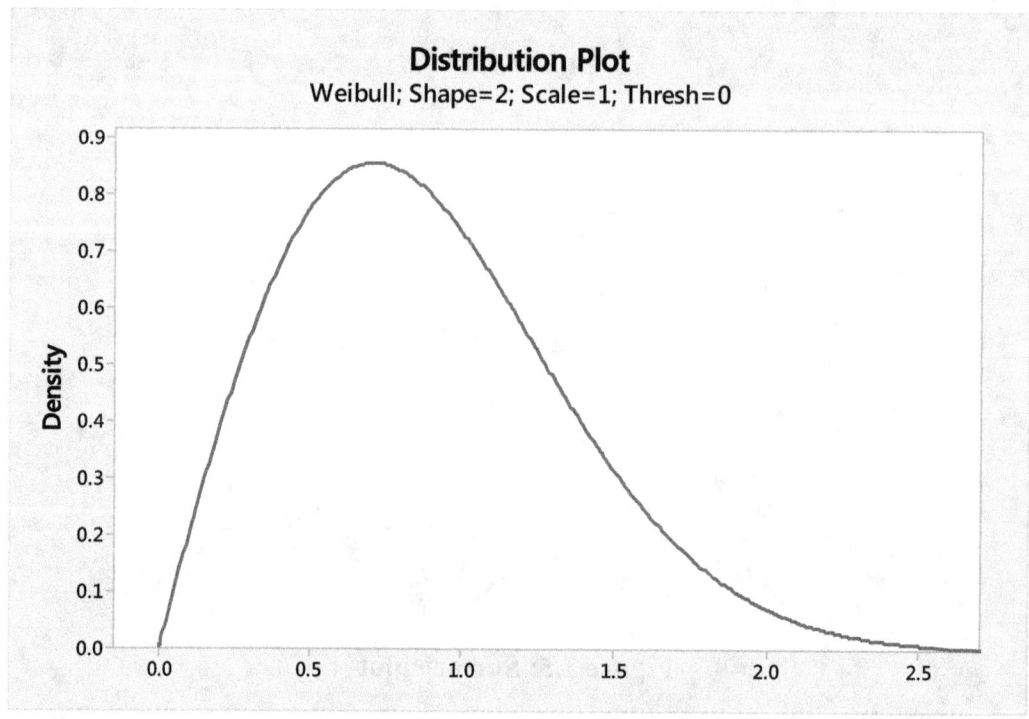

Figure 1.7: Weibull distribution

This distribution is used to determine the time-to-failure for parts or systems. The Weibull distribution changes shape as parameters change and it can even approach the shape of the standard normal distribution.

The Common Factor in These Methods This brief discussion can't cover all statistical methods used in industry, nor all of the discoverers who have contributed to statistical methods. There are, however, commonalities amongst the statistical methods presented here. These breakthroughs in statistics were not discovered by people seeking a breakthrough in *statistics*; rather, they were found by people who had a problem to solve.

Much of Gauss' work was done in the field of astronomy, and Gosset was trying to brew good beer at a low cost. Shewhart was at an industrial research laboratory, and Fisher was made his contributions to experimental design when he was attempting to interpret massive quantities of data resulting from years of agricultural experimentation.

Box was a chemist by education, but was confronted with a statistical problem and learned statistics because no other statistician was available to help him. In addition to publishing his namesake distribution, Weibull frequently published on practical engineering-related subjects, such as material strength and material fatigue.

The field of statistics has progressed over the past two centuries and we can expect that it will continue to give us new practical methods to find solutions to real-world problems. Statistics is now an essential part of the modern quality engineer's body of knowledge.

Perhaps somewhere, right now, an engineer facing a problem on the production floor is creating yet another new statistical method for solving a real-world problem.

1.3 Practical Statistical Problem Solving Using Minitab to Explore the Problem

A problem must be understood before it can be properly addressed. A thorough understanding of the problem is critical when performing a root cause analysis (RCA) and an RCA is necessary if an organization wants to implement corrective actions that truly address the root cause of the problem (Rooney & Heuvel 2004). An RCA may also be necessary for process improvement projects; it is necessary to understand the cause of the current level performance before attempts are made to improve the performance.

There are many problem solving related statistical tests that can be performed using the Minitab Statistical Software Program for exploring a problem in the early stages of an investigation. However, the actual test selected should be based upon the type of data and what needs to be understood. Figure 1.8 depicts various statistical options structured in a cause-and-effects diagram with the main branches based on characteristics that describe what the tests and methods are used for.

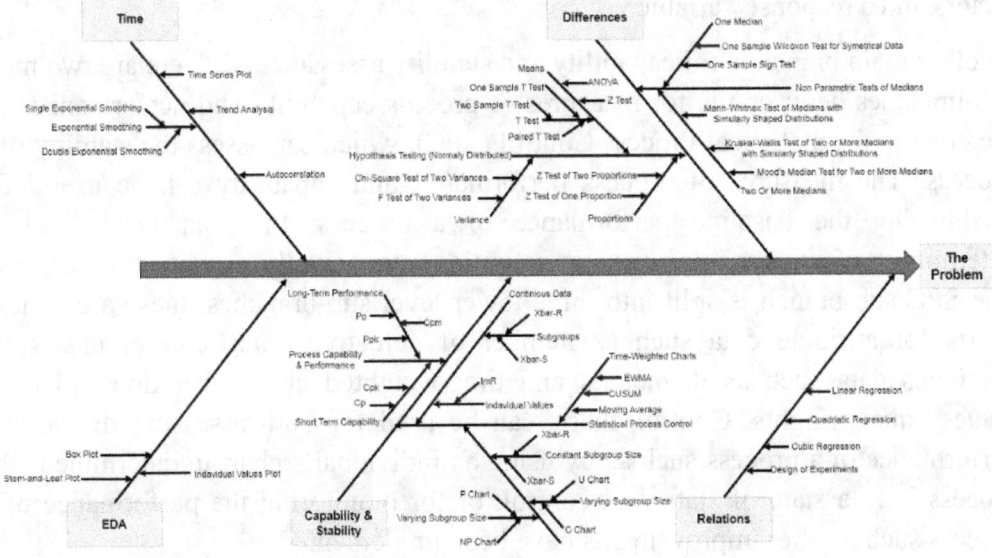

Figure 1.8: Statistical methods for problem solving

The main branch labeled "differences" is split into two high-level sub-branches; hypothesis tests that have an assumption of normality and non-parametric tests of medians. The hypothesis tests assume data is normally distributed and can be used to compare means, variances, or proportions to either a given value or to the value of a second sample. An ANOVA can be performed to compare the means of two or more samples. The non-parametric tests listed in the cause-and-effect diagram are used to compare medians; either to a specified value, or two or more medians, depending upon which test is selected. The non-parametric test provide an option when data is too skewed to use other options such as a Z test.

Time may also be of interest when exploring a problem. A time series plot can be created to show each value at the time it was produced; this may give insights into potential changes in a process. A tend analysis is much like the time series plot; however, Minitab tests for potential tends in the data such as increasing or decreasing values over time. Exponential smoothing options are available to assign exponentially decreasing weights to the values over time when attempting to predict future outcomes.

Relationships can be explored using various types of regression analysis to identify potential correlations in the data such as the relationship between the hardness of steel and the quenching time of the steel. This can be helpful when attempting to identify the factors that influence a process. Another option for understanding relationships is Design of Experiments (DoE), where experiments are planed specifically to economically explore the effects and interactions between multiple factors and a response variable.

Another main branch is for capability and stability assessments. There are two main sub-branches here; one is for measures of process capability and performance and the other is for Statistical Process Control (SPC), which can assess the stability of a process. The measures of process performance and capability can be useful for establishing the baseline performance of a process; this can be helpful in determining of process improvement activities have actually improved the process. The SPC sub-branch is split into three lower-level sub-branches; these are control charts for attribute data such as number of defective units, control charts for continues data such as diameters, and time-weighted charts that don't give all values equal weights. Control charts can be used for both assessing the current performance of a process such as by using an individual's chart to determine if the process is in a state of statistical control, or for monitoring the performance of a process such as after improvements have been implemented.

Exploratory Data Analysis (EDA) can be useful for gaining insights to the problem using graphical methods (Tukey 1977). The individual values plot is useful for simply observing the position of each value relative to the other values in a data set. For example, a box plot can be helpful when comparing the means, medians and spread of data from multiple processes. The purpose of EDA is not to form conclusions, but to gain insights that can be helpful in forming tentative hypotheses or in deciding which type of statistical test to perform.

The tests and methods presented here do not cover all available statistical tests and methods in Minitab; however, they do provide a large selection of basic options to choose from. The tools and methods presented here are helpful when exploring a problem, but their use should not be limited to problem exploration. They can also be helpful for planning and verifying improvements. For example, an individual values plot may indicate one process performs better than a comparable process and this can be confirmed using a two sample t test. The settings of the better process can be used to plan a DoE to identify the optimal settings for the two processes and the improvements can be monitored using an xBar and S chart for the two processes.

1.4 Operational Definitions: The First Step in a Statistical Analysis (Even after the Apocalypse)

Minitab Statistical Software can assist us in our analysis of data, but we must make judgments when selecting the data for an analysis. A good operational definition can be invaluable for ensuring the data we collect can be effectively analyzed using software.

Dr. W. Edwards Deming explains in *Out of the Crisis* (1989), "An operational definition of safe, round, reliable, or any other quality must be communicable, with the same meaning to vendor as to purchaser, same meaning yesterday and today to the production worker." Deming goes onto to tell us an operational definition requires a specific test, a judgment criterion, and a decision criterion to determine if something met the criteria.

The concept of operational definitions crossed my mind when I read Todd VanDerWerff's review of *Mad Max: Fury Road* at Vox (2015).

VonDerWerff presented an illustration of the percent of time individual Mad Max movies contained a chase scene based on data from the Internet Movie Data Base. I have recreated the illustration below as a bar chart using Minitab.

I first typed the data into a Minitab worksheet as shown in Figure 1.9.

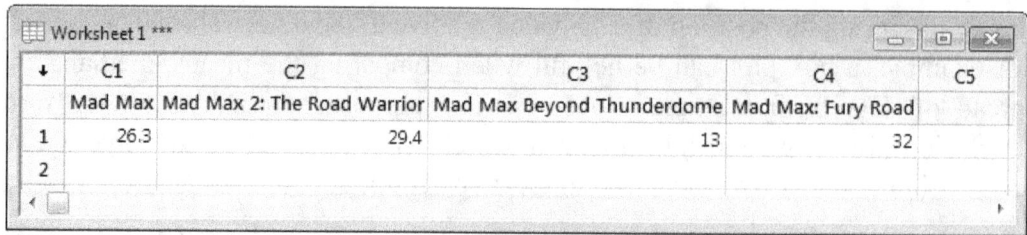

Figure 1.9: Minitab worksheet

I then stacked the data by going to **Data > Stack > Columns** and selecting columns C1-C4 (see Fig. 1.10). Next, I relabeled column C1-T as Film and column C2 as % Chase.

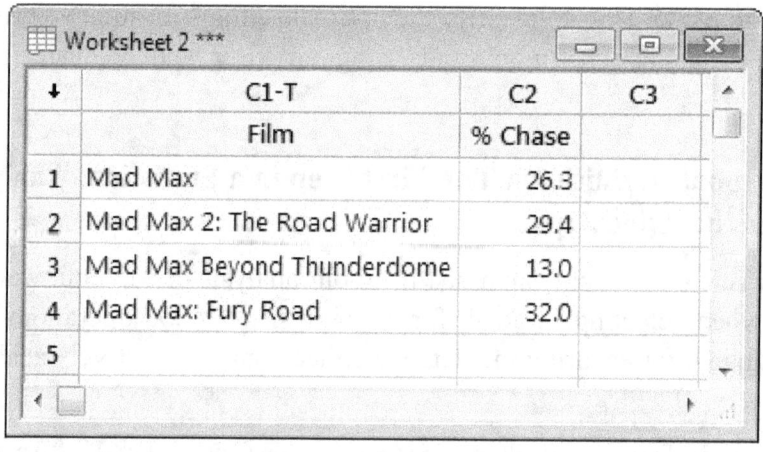

Figure 1.10: Minitab worksheet with stacked data

Then I went to **Graph > Bar Chart** and selected "Values from a table" and a "Simple" bar chart. The graph variables were % Chase and the categorical variable was Film. I clicked on the resulting bar chart and then right clicked and selected **Add > Data labels** and selected "Use labels from column" and selected % Chase. The resulting bar chart is shown in Figure 1.11.

IMPROVING PRODUCTS, SERVICES AND PROCESSES

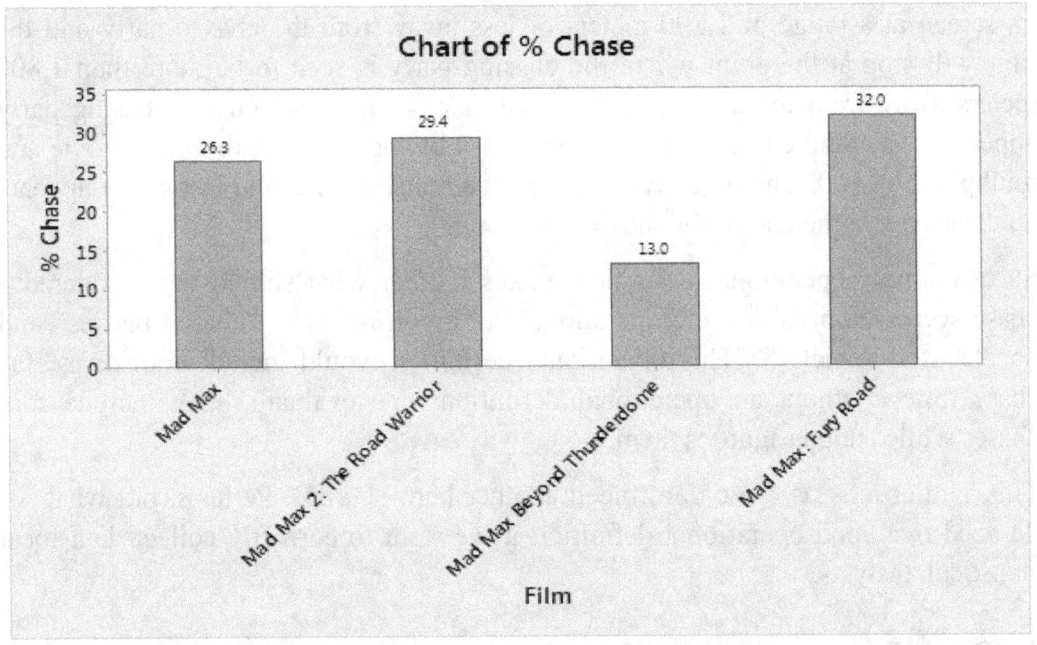

Figure 1.11: Bar chart

As a connoisseur of the Mad Max series, I was rather shocked to see that *Mad Max: Fury Road* consisted of only 32% chase scenes. I would have estimated 90-95% chase scenes! VanDerWreff explains "We're skewing toward the conservative side here and only counting scenes where the characters are in the thick of a really contentious chase, where either side might prevail." Obviously, we are using different criteria to identify a chase scene. VanDerWreff is close to an operational definition; however, "where either side might prevail" could still be open to interpretation and therefore, inadequate as an operational definition.

In *Twenty Things you Need to Know* (2009), Wheeler lists three questions that can serve as a framework for an operational definition:

1. What do you want to accomplish?
2. By what method will you accomplish your objective?
3. How will you know you have accomplished your objective?

Answering Wheeler's three questions can help us to define an operational definition for chase scenes in the latest Mad Max movie: We want to identify chase scenes in a *Mad Max: Fury Road*. We will use a calibrated stop watch capable of differentiating down to 1/100th of a second to identify the start and stop time of a chase where a chase is defined as "the time from when a chasing party first appears on screen at a range of 1,800 meters or less away from the chased party and the time will stop at the point where the chasing party is seen to be more than 1,800 meters away from the chased party or the last scene in which the chasing party appears." The total chase time is to be divided by the total length of the movie and multiplied by 100. The objective will be accomplished after the last credit appears on the screen at the end of the movie.

Such a simple operational definition makes it clear what should be considered a chase scene. Notices that the operational definition refers to "chased parties" and not "chased vehicles"? This operational definition would include foot chases as chase time. Without an operational definition, one evaluator may include foot chases while another ignores them.

Tina Turner tells us, "We don't need another hero" (1985). Perhaps, but what we do need is a good operational definition if we want to correctly collect data for a statistical analysis.

1.5 Don't Forget to Look at How You Collect Data (Whether You're Hunting Quality or Ghosts)!

In Jim Frost's article "How to Be a Ghost Hunter with a Statistical Mindset," he correctly pointed out the difficulties in distinguishing small effects from natural variation (2012). However, he did not mention the benefits of doing measurement system analysis (MSA) in both ghost hunting as depicted by his example and in the statistical study using Minitab.

In industrial settings, testing equipment is evaluated to determine if the device used to assess the factor being studied is taking accurate measurements. In other words, are you collecting data that you can trust?

By doing a statistical study without assessing your measurement tools first, you risk using a measuring device that may not be sensitive enough to measure the phenomenon under investigation (Barsalou 2015). For example, in industry this could mean measuring machined metal blocks with a variation of thousandths of a milliliter with calipers that can only measure hundredths of a millimeter. The resulting measurements might show the variation due to the calipers, but not the variation of the blocks being measured.

The same principle applies to ghost hunting with electromagnetic field (EMF) detectors. Are the EMF results due to a ghost or background EMF readings? As ghosts are not known to exist, it would be premature to conclude that they give off EMF readings.

Just as you'd want to assess the ability of the caliper to measure the metal block, an analysis should be performed on EMF detectors. A simple approach would be randomly selecting 10 houses not known to be haunted and 10 houses thought to be haunted. Naturally, each group of 10 houses should be approximately the same as each other in all factors, except that 10 are thought to be haunted. A statistical analysis could be performed using Minitab to determine if a statistically significant difference exists between EMF readings from suspected haunted houses and those from randomly selected houses.

The experimental conditions of a ghost hunt should also be considered. Ghost hunting is often done with "lights out" to increase the sensitivity of the ghost hunter's senses. But does it actually increase the sensitivity of the ghost hunter's senses? This should be empirically verified before the start of the ghost hunting. People *may* be more sensitive to unusual observations when in the dark in a place thought to be haunted. However, a person may just be subconsciously more susceptible to unusual observations because they believe they are in a haunted house.

As part of the measurement system analysis (MSA) often performed in industry, we try to ensure that there is no unacceptable operator error in our measurement results (Breyfogle 2008). The same principle could be applied to ghost hunting. Potential ghost hunters can be sent to investigate the 20 houses used to assess our EMF detectors.

Blinding and randomization should be used to increase accuracy. An experimenter should randomly select the order in which the 20 houses would be investigated and a second person who is unaware of the status of each house should give the ghost hunter the list of addresses and a check list to identify any unusual observations that are made in the houses. This ensures the second experimenter does not inadvertently give the ghost hunter clues about the status of the houses. The houses should all be investigated at the same time of night and in the dark.

At the end of the study the checklist from the ghost hunters would be analyzed using statistical software to determine if a statistically significant difference exists between unusual observations made in suspected haunted houses and those in randomly selected houses.

If the results show no difference between unusual observations from known haunted houses and randomly selected houses, it could be an indication that the methodology for ghost hunting should be revised. The results of EMF detectors in haunted houses should also be called into question if the analysis shows no difference in results between known haunted houses and randomly selected houses.

To sum up, just like as do in industry, ghost hunters should confirm their methodology works before gathering their data. Then they can improve their methodology if it is not sufficient, or be more open to Frost's null hypothesis: Ghosts do not exist.

CHAPTER 2

Exploring Data Graphically

This chapter covers graphical methods and Exploratory Data Analysis, which is used to explore a problem or dataset graphically. The first section presents an idea and then uses graphs of data to determine if further study is warranted. The concept of Star Trek characters in redshirts dying more often is investigated using Bayes theorem to determine if they really die more often or if it is because there are more of them; along the way, the use of various types of graphs in Minitab is explained.

Various statistical distributions are presented and explained. In addition to introducing the distributions, this chapter also describes how to use Minitab to identify the distribution of a data set. Creating a probability plot by hand is also explained. The probability plot is used to determine if data follows the normal distribution; which is often a requirement for many statistical methods. Assessing the normality of data using Minitab is also presented.

2.1 Exploratory Data Analysis: The First (and Sometimes Last) Step

A good way to begin researching a topic is with Exploratory Data Analysis (EDA). In his 1977 book *Exploratory Data Analysis,* John Tukey suggested using EDA to collect and analyze data—not to confirm a hypothesis, but to *form* a hypothesis that could later be confirmed through other methods (1977).

In some cases, EDA can even eliminate the need for a more in-depth hypothesis test. Here's a case in point.

When I heard about the new *Star Trek* movie, I had started to complain to anybody who would listen (which was not many people) that director J. J. Abrams had used such a young cast in the 2009 *Star Trek* film.

With a tentative hypothesis of "the new *Star Trek* films use very young actors and actresses compared to the older Star Trek series," I decided to look into this further. The first thing I did was collect data to use later in boxplots, which are a part of Tukey's EDA.

Collecting Data for the Exploratory Analysis I needed to determine the ages at which each main *Star Trek* actor first appeared; however, before I started looking for ages, I needed a method to determine whom I should consider as a main character in each series. To select the actors to consider I went to www.StarTrek.com (2017) and observed which characters were listed for each *Star Trek* series. This way I avoided biasing my results by selecting older or younger crewmembers who may not have had as much relevance as others.

The tables below list the characters and the episode or movie in which they first appeared. The name of the actor playing each character is then listed, and their year of birth as determined by viewing their entry at the Internet Movie Database (2017). To determine the person's age, the date of birth was subtracted from the year of first appearance. This resulted in rough calculations which could be wrong by a year, because month of birth and month of first appearance were not considered. The results are shown in Tables 2.1 through 2.6.

Name	Character	First Appeared in	Birth Year	1st Appearance	Age +/- 1 year
William Shatner	James T. Kirk	The Man Trap	1931	1966	35
Leonard Nimoy	Spock	The Man Trap	1931	1966	35
DeForest Kelley	Leonard "Bones" McCoy	The Man Trap	1920	1966	46
James Doohan	Montgomery "Scotty" Scott	The Man Trap	1920	1966	46
George Takei	Sulu	The Man Trap	1937	1966	29

| Nichelle Nichols | Uhura | The Man Trap | 1932 | 1966 | 34 |
| Walter Koenig | Pavel Andreievich Checkov | Amok Time | 1936 | 1967 | 31 |

Table 2.1: Star Trek: The Original Series

Name	Character	First appeared in	Birth Year	1st Appearance	Age +/- 1 year
Patrick Stewart	Jean-Luc Picard	Encounter at Farpoint	1940	1987	47
Jonathan Frakes	Will Riker	Encounter at Farpoint	1952	1987	35
Brent Spiner	Data	Encounter at Farpoint	1949	1987	38
Levar Burton	Geordi La Forge	Encounter at Farpoint	1957	1987	30
Michael Dorn	Worf	Encounter at Farpoint	1952	1987	35
Marina Sirtits	Deana Troi	Encounter at Farpoint	1955	1987	32
Gates McFadden	Beverly Crusher	Encounter at Farpoint	1949	1987	38
Wil Wheaton	Wesley Crusher	Encounter at Farpoint	1972	1987	15

Table 2.2: Star Trek: The Next Generation

Name	Character	First appeared in	Birth Year	1st Appearance	Age +/- 1 year
Avery Brooks	Benjamin Sisko	Emissary	1948	1993	45
Nan Visitor	Kira Nerys	Emissary	1957	1993	36
Rene Auberjonois	Odo	Emissary	1940	1993	53
Alexander Siddig	Julian Bashir	Emissary	1965	1993	28
Colm Meany	Miles	Emissary	1953	1993	40

	O'Brien				
Terry Farrell	Jadzia Dax	Emissary	1963	1993	30
Armin Shimerman	Quark	Emissary	1949	1993	44
Cirroc Lofton	Jake Sisko	Emissary	1978	1993	15
Michael Dorn	Worf	The Way of the Warrior	1952	1995	46
Nicole de Boer	Ezri Dax	Image in the Sand	1970	1998	28

Table 2.3: Star Trek: Deep Space Nine

Name	Character	First appeared in	Birth Year	1st Appearance	Age +/- 1 year
Kate Mulgrew	Kathryn Janeway	Caretaker	1955	1995	40
Robert Beltran	Chakotay	Caretaker	1953	1995	42
Tim Russ	Tuvok	Caretaker	1956	1995	39
Robert Duncan McNeill	Tom Paris	Caretaker	1964	1995	31
Roxann Dawson	B'Elanna Torres	Caretaker	1958	1995	37
Garrett Wang	Harry Kim	Caretaker	1968	1995	27
Robert Picardo	The Doctor	Caretaker	1953	1995	42
Ethan Phillips	Neelix	Caretaker	1955	1995	40
Jennifer Lien	Kes	Caretaker	1974	1995	21
Jerry Ryan	Seven of Nine	Scorpion: Part 2	1968	1997	29

Table 2.4: Star Trek: Voyager

Name	Character	First appeared in	Birth Year	1st Appearance	Age +/- 1 year
Scott Bakula	Jonathan	Broken	1954	2001	47

	Archer	Bow: Part 1			
Jolene Blalock	T'pol	Broken Bow: Part 1	1975	2001	26
Connor Trinneer	Charles "Trip" Tucker III	Broken Bow: Part 1	1969	2001	32
Dominic Keating	Malcom Reed	Broken Bow: Part 1	1962	2001	39
John Billingsley	Phlox	Broken Bow: Part 1	1960	2001	41
Linda Park	Hoshi Sato	Broken Bow: Part 1	1978	2001	23
Anthony Montgomery	Travis Mayweather	Broken Bow: Part 1	1971	2001	30

Table 2.5: Star Trek: Enterprise

Name	Character	First appeared in	Birth Year	1st Appearance	Age +/- 1 year
Chris Pine	James T. kirk	Star Trek (2009)	1980	2009	29
Zachary Quinto	Spock	Star Trek (2009)	1977	2009	32
Karl Urban	Leonard "Bones" McCoy	Star Trek (2009)	1972	2009	37
Zoe Saldana	Nyota Uhura	Star Trek (2009)	1978	2009	31
Simon Pegg	Montgomery "Scotty" Scott	Star Trek (2009)	1970	2009	39
John Cho	Hukaru Sulu	Star Trek (2009)	1972	2009	37
Anton Yelchin	Pavel Andreievich Checkov	Star Trek (2009)	1989	2009	20

Table 2.6: Star Trek (2009)

I then took the data from tables 1-6 and made Table 2.7, which I coped into Minitab.

Star Trek: TOS	Star Trek: TNG	Star Trek: DS9	Star Trek: Voyager	Star Trek: Enterprise	Star Trek (2009)
35	47	45	40	47	29
35	35	36	42	26	32
46	38	53	39	32	37
46	30	28	31	39	31
29	35	40	37	41	39
34	32	30	27	23	37
31	38	44	42	30	20
	15	15	40		
		46	21		
		28	29		

Table 2.7: Age and series/film of first appearance

EDA: Interpreting the Data with a Boxplot Simply looking at the results in tables 1 through 6 led to me suspect my hypothesis may have been incorrect, but I still proceeded to create a Minitab boxplot with the data. I created a box plot by going to **Graph** > **Boxplot** and selecting **Multiple Y's Simple**. I entered the columns containing the data then right-clicked on the resulting boxplot. I selected **Add** > **Data display** and then placed a checkmark next to "Mean symbol" so I could observe the means. The resulting boxplot is shown in Fig. 2.1.

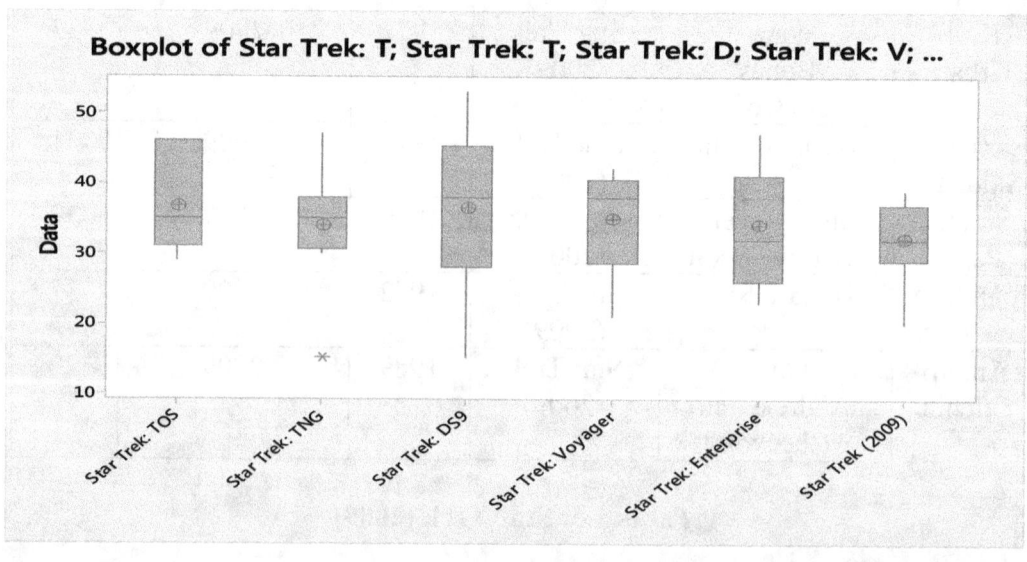

Figure 2.1: Boxplots

The boxplot depicts the ages of the actors and actresses in each Star Trek series as well as in the 2009 reboot. The rectangular boxes represent the middle 50% of each data set and the vertical lines on top of the rectangular boxes represent the upper 25% of the data. The vertical lines on the bottom of the rectangular boxes represent the lower 25% of the data—except in the case of outliers. Outliers are unusually large or small observations and are represented by an asterisk. There is only one outlier in this boxplot, and that is Will Wheaton as Wesley Crusher in Star Trek: TNG.

The symbol that looks like a plus sign inside of a small circle is used to represent the average of the data set. The average age of actors and actresses in the 2009 reboot is 33.57 years, and this is just slightly lower than Star Trek: TNG, which had an average of 33.75 years of age. The highest average age was for Star Trek: TOS with an average of 36.57.

What truly stands out is that the highest value of every boxplot is higher than the highest value of the 2009 reboot. The mean of the 2009 film seems to be lower than any of the others, but I would need to perform a hypothesis test to determine if it is statistically significant. Lower ages in the reboot would make sense as it would not be plausible to use actors or actresses in their 50s or 60s to portray people who are still attending Star Fleet Academy.

The hypothesis that originally started this was "the new Star Trek films use very young actors and actresses compared to the older Star Trek series," and a look at the boxplots in Figure one show that this may be the case, but it is unclear so I should proceed on to confirmation testing to look into this further. So far, I don't owe director J. J. Abrams an apology.

Exploratory Data Analysis Raises New Questions Even a hypothesis that was discarded after performing EDA can lead to the...um...*next generation* of hypotheses, and new insights. For example, my new hypothesis could be, "The actors and actresses in Star Trek are not getting younger; I am getting older." The new hypothesis could also be explored with EDA prior to moving on to more robust methods. However, in such a case, I would not investigate my new hypothesis. I would rather just change the subject.

In the actual example I would move onto an ANOVA to determine if one or more means differs from the others.

2.2 Keep your Redshirt on: A Bayesian Exploration

The idea of red-shirted characters being frequently killed in *Star Trek: The Original Series* has become a pop culture cliché. But is wearing a redshirt in Star Trek as hazardous as it is thought to be? To find out, casualty figures for the

PRACTICAL STATISTICAL METHODS FOR QUALITY

Starship Enterprise were compiled using the casualty list provided by Memory Alpha (2017) (see Table 2.8).

Uniform Color	Color's Meaning	Casualties	Comments on the Data
Blue	Science and medical	7	
Gold	Command and helm	9	Includes Lee Kelso and Gary Mitchell who wore the old style chartreuse command and helm uniform. Also includes O'Neil, whose uniform was not listed, but can be observed in the episode The Galileo Seven.
Red	Operations, engineering and security	24	
Unknown	n/a	15	Includes nine killed by the galactic barrier in Where no Man has Gone Before, three Rigelian fever victims from Requiem for Methuselah, and one unknown casualty of the dikironium cloud creature in Obsession. Also includes Sam and Barnhart who were not in standard uniforms when they died.

Table 2.8: Enterprise NCC 1701 casualties from episodes aired between September 8, 1966 and June 03, 1969 based on casualty figures from Memory Alpha.

Note: Table does not contain casualties from the Mirror Universe or anybody killed and resurrected during an episode

A pie chart was created using Minitab to graphically view the data. It is obvious from the pie chart in Figure 1 that redshirts suffer most of the casualties. However, raw casualty figures are not very informative without knowing how many people were in each uniform. According to the a set of Enterprise blueprints endorsed by Paramount Pictures, the Enterprise's 430 crew members consisted of 55 command and helm personnel, 136 science and medical personnel and 239 engineering, operations and security personnel (Franz Joseph Designs 1975). This means 16.4% of casualties were in command and helm, 5.4% were in science and medical and 10.0% were in operations, engineering and security. Of the remaining 27.3% of casualties, 12 were killed by contact with the galactic barrier or Rigelian fever, which could have affected personnel regardless of duty assignments (see Table 2.9).

Uniform Color	Casualties	Total Population	Casualties as Percent of Population
Blue	7	136	5.1
Gold	9	55	13.4
Red	24	239	10
Unknown	15	n/a	n/a
Total	55	430	12.8

Table 2.9: Enterprise NCC 1701 casualties by uniform color.

Note: There were 18 security department casualties out of the total of 24 redshirt casualties. This means the security department with 90 people lost 20% of its members

Go to **Graph > Pie Chart** and select "Chart values from a table." Use Uniform Color as the "Categorical variable" and Casualties as the "Summary variable." Right click on the resulting pie chart (see Fig. 2.2) and select **Add > Slice Labels**. Place a checkmark next to "Category name" and "Frequency."

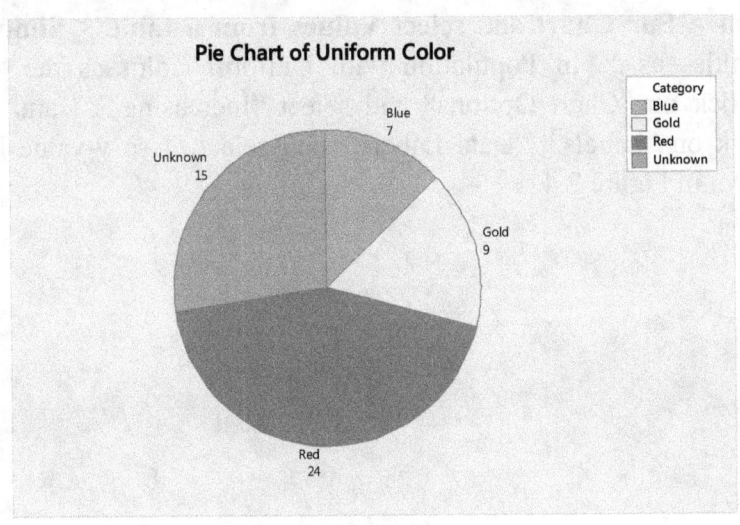

Figure 2.2: Casualties by Uniform Color

Go to **Graph > Bar Chart** and select "Values from a table" and **One column of values > Simple**. Enter Casualties and Total Population as the "Graph variables" and Uniform Color as the "Categorical variable." Click on "Chart options" and select "Increasing Y" and "Show Y as percent" and click **OK** one time. Then click on "Multiple Graphs" and select "In separate panels of the same graph." The resulting graph is depicted in Figure 2.3.

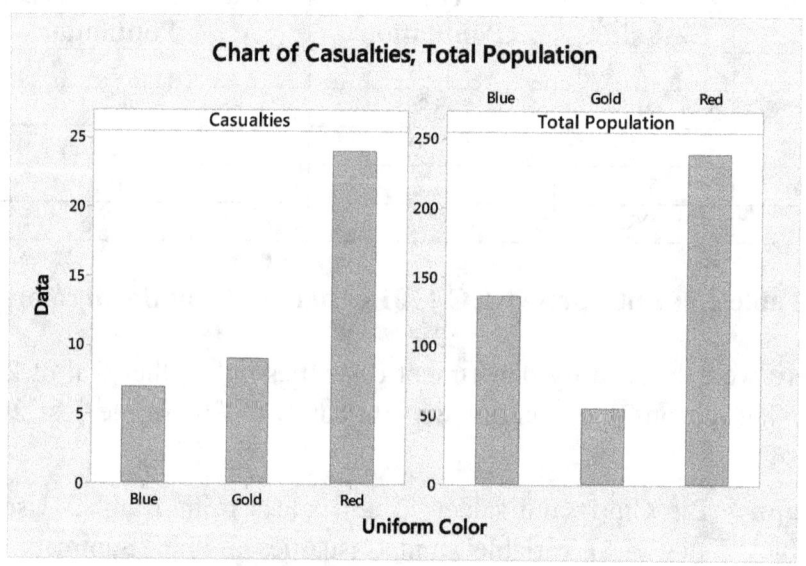

Figure 2.3: Chart of Casualties and Populations

Go to **Graph > Bar Chart** and select **Values from a table < Simple** and then select Casualties as % of Population with Uniform Color as the "Categorical variable." Click on "Chart Options" and select "Increasing Y" and Show Y as Percent. Click on "Labels," "Data Labels," and select "Use y-value labels." The result is shown in Figure 2.4.

IMPROVING PRODUCTS, SERVICES AND PROCESSES

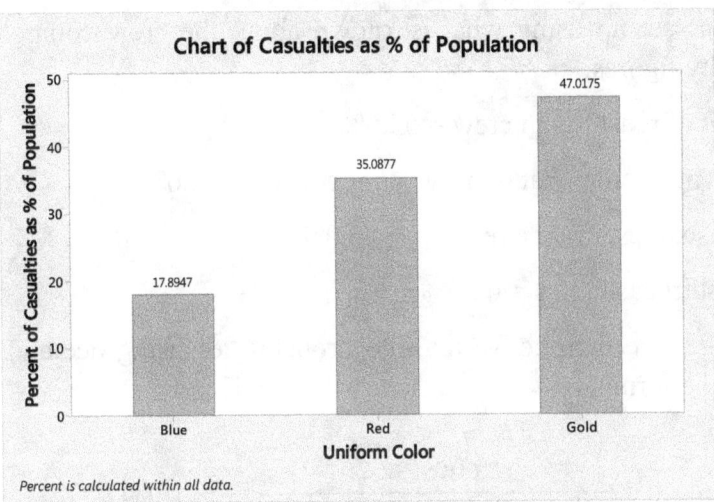

Figure 2.4: Chart of Casualties as a Percentage of Each department

Based on an analysis of casualties that considers the overall total number of personnel in each color of uniform, wearing a redshirt may not be the automatic death sentence that it is popularly considered to be. On the other hand, 18 of the redshirt casualties were security personnel out of a total population of 90; 20% of the security department were casualties. Although wearing a redshirt may not of itself be particularly hazardous, personnel in a redshirt who are members of the security department should expect to pay a high premium on their life insurance.

Using what is known about Enterprise crew and casualty figures, suppose an Enterprise crew member has been killed. Discarding the 15 unknown casualties, redshirts consist of 60.0% of all fatalities where the uniform color is known; blue and gold uniforms are the remaining 40.0% of casualties. Redshirts are only 52.0% of the entire crew, but 60.0% of casualties, so what is the probability that the latest casualty was wearing a redshirt? The Enterprise often visits Starbases and takes on new crew members, so we assume sampling with replacement. Otherwise, the population size would change every time a crew member is killed.

Bayes' theorem, also known as Bayes' rule, can be used to solve this. Bayes' theorem solves for P(A|B), where P(A|B) is the probability of A given the B has happened (Larson and Marx 1990). In this situation, that would be the probability that somebody is wearing a red shirt (A) if they are a casualty (B).

$$P(A|B) = \frac{P(B|A)P(A)}{P(B|A)P(A)+P(B|\sim A)P(\sim A)}$$

PRACTICAL STATISTICAL METHODS FOR QUALITY

The formula is set up using what is known about the crew composition and the known casualty figures.

$P(A)$ = Percent of redshirts in crew = 52.0%

$P(\sim A)$ = Percent of crew that don't wear a redshirt = 48.0%

$P(B|\sim A)$ = Casualties not in a redshirt = 40.0%

$P(B|A)$ = Redshirt casualties = 60.0%

The percentages are then converted into probabilities using decimal notation and plugged into the formula:

$$\frac{(0.600)(0.520)}{(0.600)(0.520)+(0.400)(0.480)} = 0.619$$

There is a 61.9% chance that any given casualty is wearing a redshirt. This really does not help the insurance premiums of operations, engineering and security personnel. Three departments wear redshirts so it may be worthwhile to take a deeper look at the data to determine if a wearing a redshirt is as hazardous as it appears to be. According to table 2, the security department suffered 18 out of the 24 red shirt deaths. What does Bayes' theorem say about this?

Suppose a crew member finds a casualty with a redshirt. This may or may not be a member of security. Redshirts in security are 75.0% of all redshirt casualties and other redshirts are only 25%. However, security is only 37.7% of all people in a redshirt. How likely is the casualty to be a member of security?

$P(A)$ = Percentage of redshirts in security = 37.7%

$P(\sim A)$ = Redshirts that are not in security = 62.3%

$P(B|\sim A)$ = Redshirt casualties not in security = 25.0%

$P(B|A)$ = Redshirts casualties in security = 75.0%

The probabilities are then entered into the formula:

$$\frac{(0.750)(0.377)}{(0.750)(0.377)+(0.250)(0.623)} = 0.645$$

There is a 64.5% chance that any given casualty in a redshirt is a member of security. We can also conclude there is only a 35.5% chance that any casualty in a redshirt is not a member of security. This is in spite of security being only 37.7% of the entire population of redshirts. So what does this mean for red-shirted crew members not in security? Remember, security, operations and engineering wear redshirts. The 15 unknown crew members are not included in this calculation.

$P(A)$ = Percentage of crew members in operations and engineering (redshirt, but not in security) = 34.7%

$P(\sim A)$ = Percentage of crew members not in operations or engineering = 65.3%

$P(B|\sim A)$ = Casualties not in operations and engineering = 85.0%

$P(B|A)$= Casualties in operation and engineering = 15.0%

The probabilities are plugged into the formula:

$$\frac{(0.150)(0.347)}{(0.150)(0.347)+(0.850)(0.653)} = 0.086$$

In spite of wearing a redshirt, there is only an 8.6% chance of a member of the operations or engineering departments becoming a casualty. These personnel should ensure that their life insurance plans are based on their departments and not their uniform color.

Although Enterprise crew members in redshirts suffer many more casualties than crew members in other uniforms, they suffer fewer casualties than crew members in gold uniforms when the entire population size is considered. Only 10% of the entire redshirt population was lost during the three year run of Star Trek. This is less than the 13.4% of goldshirts, but more than the 5.1% of blueshirts. What is truly hazardous is not wearing a redshirt, but being a member of the security department. The red-shirted members of security were only 20.9% of the entire crew, but there is a 61.9% chance that the next casualty is in a redshirt and 64.5% chance this red-shirted victim is a member of the security department. The remaining redshirts, operations and engineering make up the largest single population, but only have an 8.6% chance of being a casualty.

Red uniform shirts are safe, as long as the wearer is not in the security department.

2.3 A Field Guide to Statistical Distributions

The old saying "if it walks like a duck, quacks like a duck and looks like a duck, then it must be a duck" may be appropriate in bird watching; however, the same idea can't be applied when observing a statistical distribution. The dedicated ornithologist is often armed with binoculars and a field guide to the local birds and this should be sufficient. A statologist (I just made the word up, feel free to use it) on the other hand, is ill-equipped for the visual identification of his or her targets.

Normal, Student's t, Chi-Square, and F Distributions Notice the upper two distributions in figure 1. The normal distribution and student's t distribution may appear similar. However, the standard normal distribution is calculated using n and student's t distribution is calculated using n-1. This may appear to be a minor difference, but when n is small, student's t distribution displays much more peakedness. Student's t distribution approaches the normal distribution as the sample size increases, but it never truly matches the shape of the normal distribution (Freedman, Pisani, and Purves 1978).

Observe the Chi-square and F distribution in the lower half of Figure 2.5. The shapes of the distributions can vary and even the most astute observer will not be able to differentiate between them by eye. Many distributions can be sneaky like that. It is a part of their nature that we must accept as we can't change it.

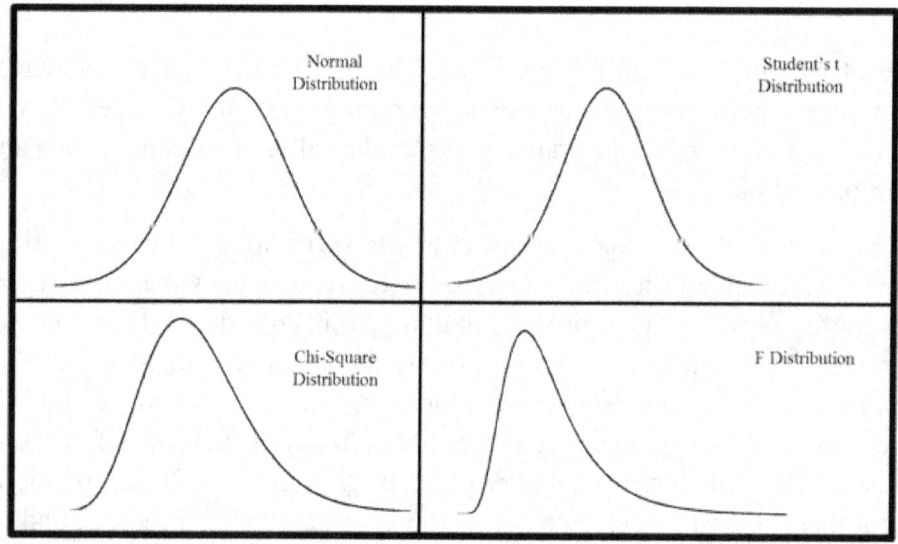

Figure 2.5: Normal, Student's t, Chi-Square, and F Distributions

Binomial, Hypergeometric, Poisson, and Laplace Distributions Notice the distributions illustrated in Figure 2.6. A bird watcher may suddenly encounter four birds sitting in a tree; a quick check of a reference book may help to determine that they are all of a different species. The same can't always be said for statistical distributions. Observe the binomial distribution, hypergeometric distribution and Poisson distribution; we can't even be sure the three are not the same distribution! If they are together with a Laplace distribution, an observer may conclude "one of these does not appear to be the same as the others." But they *are* all different, which our eyes alone may fail to tell us.

IMPROVING PRODUCTS, SERVICES AND PROCESSES

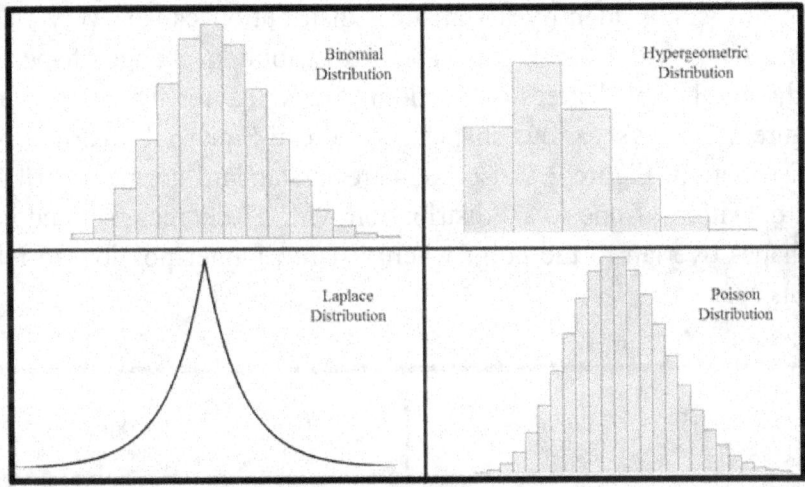

Figure 2.6: Binomial, Hypergeometric, Poisson, and Laplace Distributions

Weibull, Cauchy, Loglogistic, and Logistic Distributions Suppose we observe the four distributions in Figure 2.7. What are they? Could you tell if they were not labeled? We must identify them correctly before we can do anything with them. One is a Weibull distribution, but all four could conceivably be various Weibull distributions. The shape of the Weibull distribution varies based upon the shape parameter (κ) and scale parameter (λ) (O'Connor and Kleyner 2012). The Weibull distribution is a useful, but potentially devious distribution that can be much like the double-barred finch, which may be mistaken for an owl upon first glance.

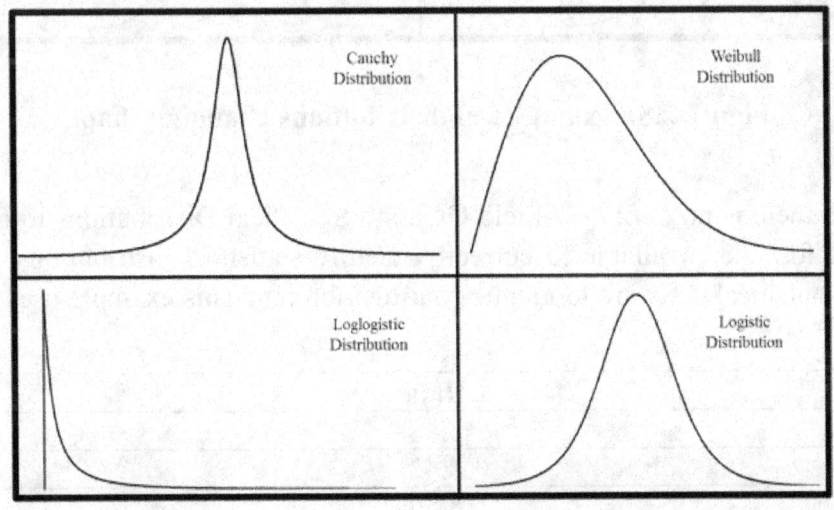

Figure 2.7: Weibull, Cauchy, Loglogistic, and Logistic Distributions

Attempting to visually identify a statistical distribution can be very risky. Many distributions such as the Chi-Square and F distribution change shape drastically based on the number of degrees of freedom (Meek, Taylor, Dunning, and Klafehn 1987). Figure 2.8 shows various shapes for the Chi-Square, F distribution and the Weibull distribution. Figure 2.8 also compares a standard normal distribution with a standard deviation of one to a t distribution with 27 degrees of freedom; notices how the shapes overlap to the point where it is no longer possible to tell the two distributions apart.

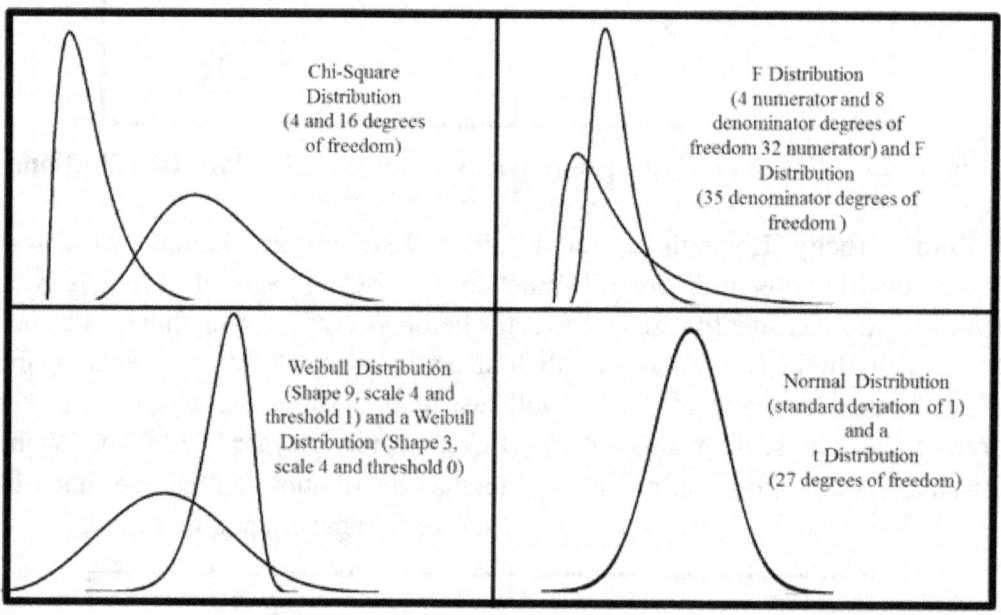

Figure 2.8: **Examples of distributions changing shape**

Although there is no definitive Field Guide to Statistical Distributions to guide us, there are formulas available to correctly identify statistical distributions. We can also use statistical software to identify our distribution. This example uses the data in Table 2.10.

Data
5.48
8.42
8.59
7.13
9.4
4.8

8.27
3.3
5.63
3.28
2.71
9.96
14.28
6.78
6.68
1.23
11.4
4.05
9.37
9.76
2.7
5.41
8.7
7.97
8.95

Table 2.10: Data

Go to **Stat > Quality Tools > Individual Distribution Identification** and enter the column containing the data and the subgroup size; use subgroup size 1 if the data was not collected in subgroups. The results can be observed in either the session window (see Fig. 2.9) or the graphical outputs shown in Figures 2.10 through 2.13 were we would reject the distributions with low p-scores. In this case, we can conclude we are observing a Normal distribution based on the p value of 0.595.

PRACTICAL STATISTICAL METHODS FOR QUALITY

Descriptive Statistics

N	N*	Mean	StDev	Median	Minimum	Maximum	Skewness	Kurtosis
25	0	6.97001	3.10834	7.12732	1.23165	14.2769	0.133853	-0.145201

Box-Cox transformation: λ = 1

Goodness of Fit Test

Distribution	AD	P	LRT P
Normal	0.286	0.595	
Box-Cox Transformation	0.286	0.595	
Lognormal	0.833	0.027	
3-Parameter Lognormal	0.321	*	0.021
Exponential	3.466	<0.003	
2-Parameter Exponential	2.483	<0.010	0.006
Weibull	0.354	>0.250	
3-Parameter Weibull	0.329	0.491	0.845
Smallest Extreme Value	0.507	0.201	
Largest Extreme Value	0.523	0.186	
Gamma	0.565	0.166	
3-Parameter Gamma	0.597	*	0.316
Logistic	0.333	>0.250	
Loglogistic	0.694	0.041	
3-Parameter Loglogistic	0.334	*	0.062

ML Estimates of Distribution Parameters

Distribution	Location	Shape	Scale	Threshold
Normal*	6.97001		3.10834	
Box-Cox Transformation*	6.97001		3.10834	
Lognormal*	1.81664		0.56073	
3-Parameter Lognormal	3.96723		0.05754	-45.95552
Exponential			6.97001	
2-Parameter Exponential			5.97745	0.99255
Weibull		2.45751	7.85445	
3-Parameter Weibull		2.62721	8.30014	-0.40182
Smallest Extreme Value	8.50704		3.08288	
Largest Extreme Value	5.46218		2.81175	
Gamma		4.16004	1.67547	
3-Parameter Gamma		421.59266	0.14822	-55.98113
Logistic	6.99488		1.77472	
Loglogistic	1.88223		0.30222	
3-Parameter Loglogistic	6.54800		0.00254	-690.85791

* Scale: Adjusted ML estimate

Figure 2.9: Minitab session window for individual distribution identification

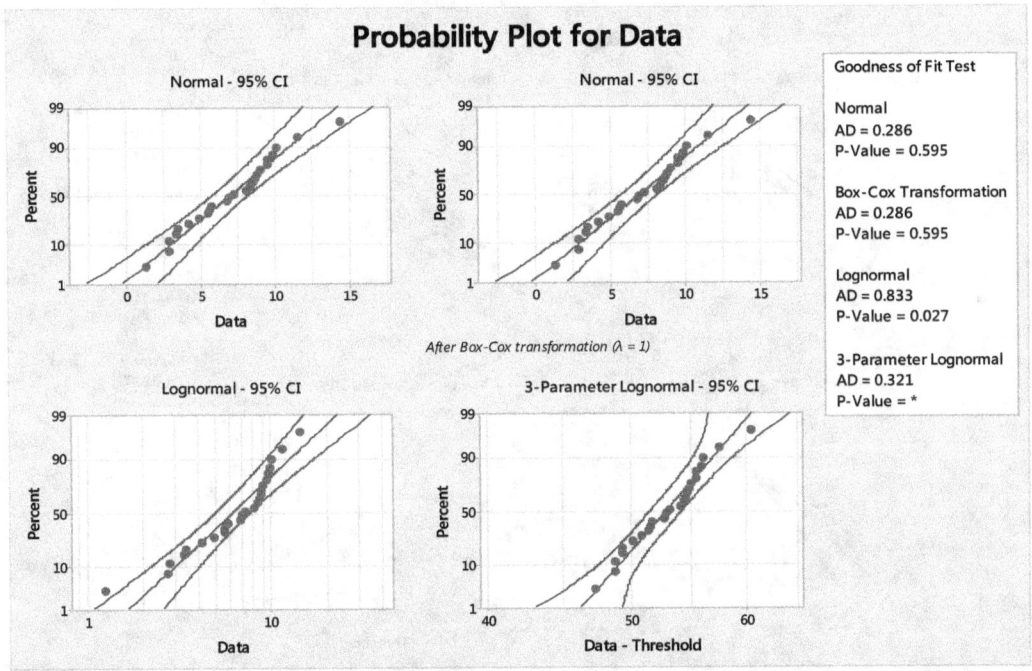

Figure 2.10: Probability plot of Normal, transformed, lognormal, and 3-parameter lognormal distributions

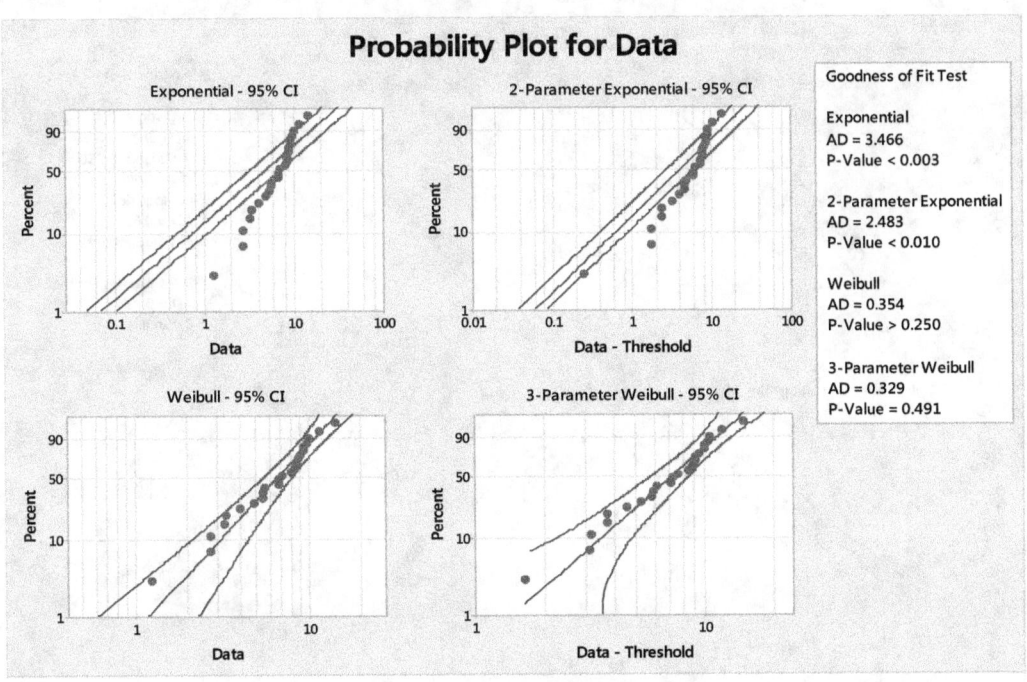

Figure 2.11: Exponential, 2-parameter exponential, Weibull, and 3-parameter Weibull distributions

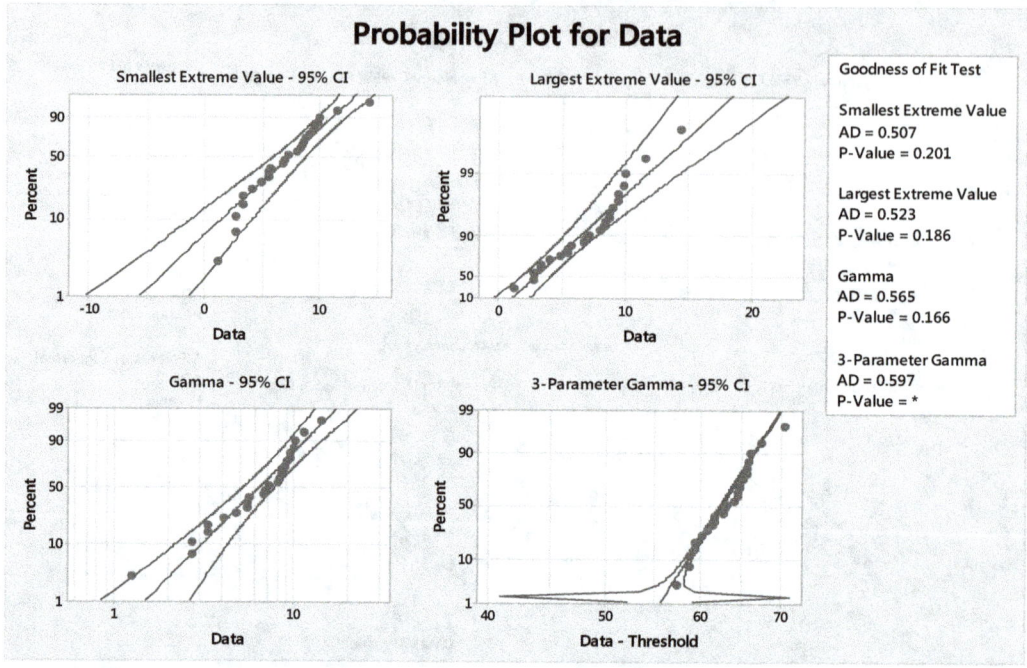

Figure 2.12: Smallest extreme value, largest extreme values, Gama, and 3-parameter Gama distributions

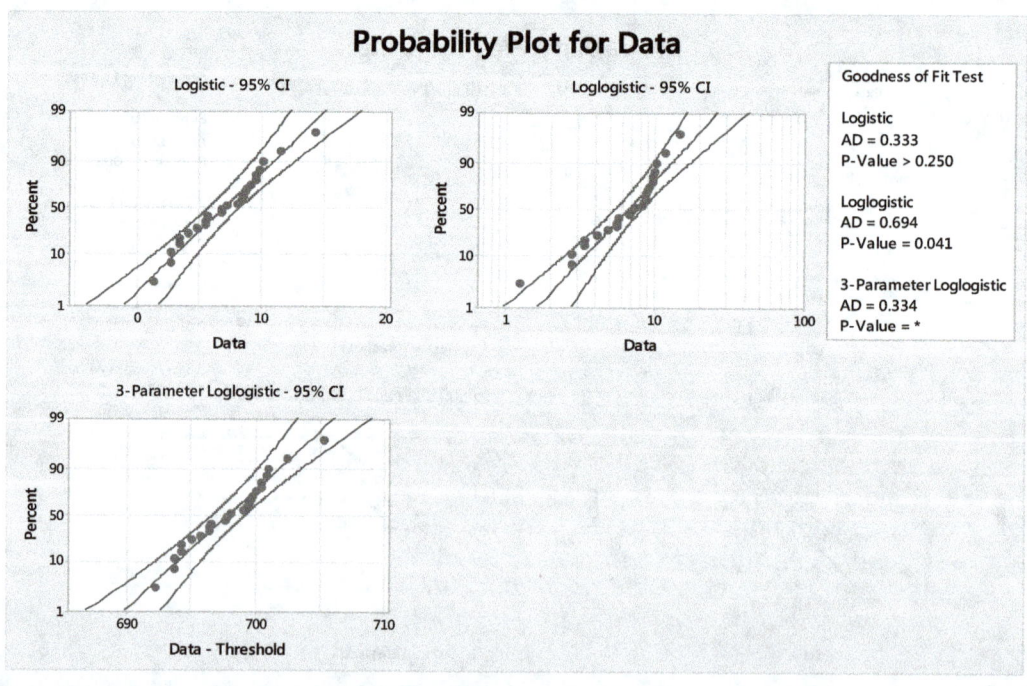

Figure 2.13: Logistic, loglogistic, and 3-parameter loglogistic distributions

2.4 Pencils and Plots: Assessing the Normality of Data

Many statistical tests assume the data being tested came from a normal distribution. Violating the assumption of normality can result in incorrect conclusions. For example, a Z test may indicate a new process is more efficient than an older process when this is not true. This could result in a capital investment for equipment that actually results in higher costs in the long run.

Capability studies require either normally distributed data or a transformation must be performed on the data (Borror 2009). It would be very risky to accept a capability value with data that violated the assumption of normality.

What can we do if the assumption of normality is critical to so many statistical methods? We can construct a probability plot to test this assumption.

Those of us who are a bit old-fashioned can construct a probability plot by hand, by plotting the order values (j) against the observed cumulative frequency (j- 0.5/n) (Montgomery, Runger, and Hubele 2001). Using the numbers 16, 21, 20, 19, 18 and 15, we would construct a normal probability plot by first creating the table shown below in Table 2.11.

j	Xj	$(j – 0.5)/6$
1	15	0.158
2	16	0.325
3	18	0.492
4	19	0.658
5	20	0.825
6	21	0.992

Table 2.11: Probability plot data

We then plot the results as shown in the Figure 2.14.

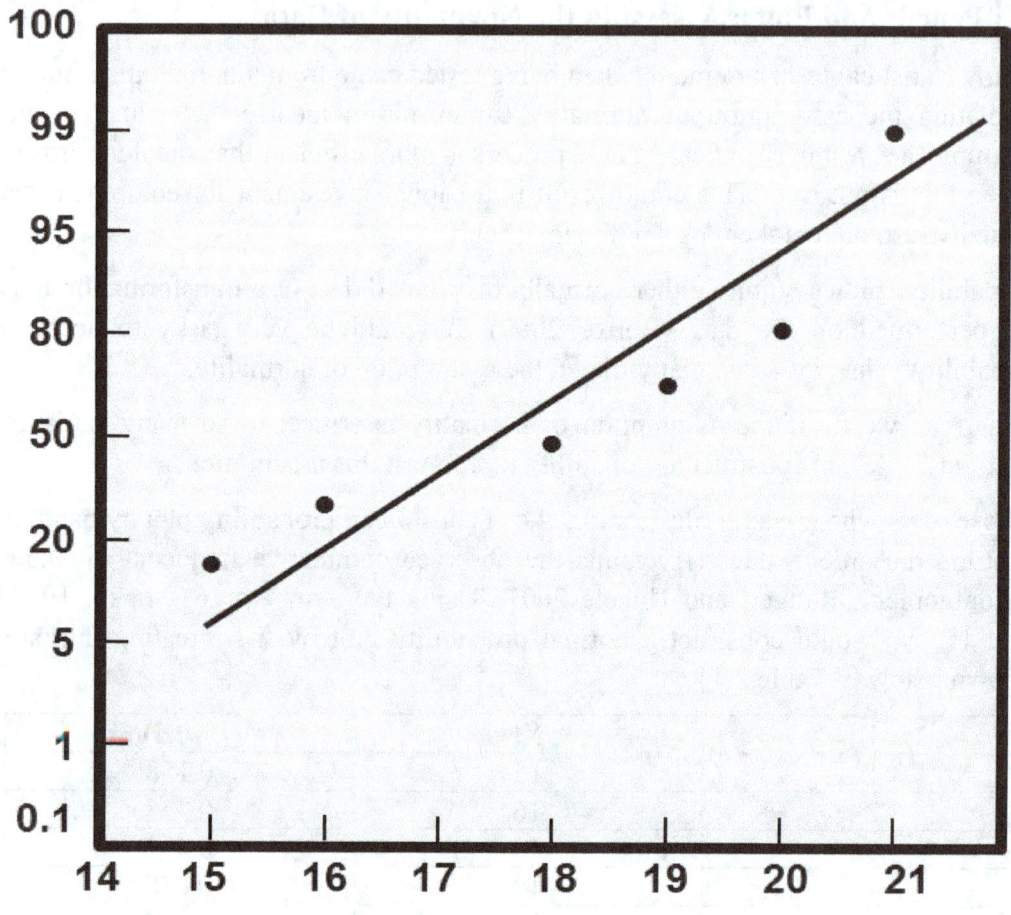

Figure 2.14: Probability plot

That's fine for a small data set, but nobody wants to plot hundreds or thousands of data points by hand. Fortunately, we can also use Minitab Statistical Software to assess the normality of data. Minitab uses the Anderson-Darling test, which compares the actual distribution to a theoretical normal distribution. Anderson-Darling test's null hypothesis is "The distribution is normal."

Anderson-Darling test:

H_0: The data follow a normal distribution.

H_a: The data don't follow a normal distribution.

Test statistic: $A^2 = -N - S$, where

$$S = \sum_{i=1}^{N} \frac{(2i-1)}{BN} \left[\text{Ln} f(Y_i) + \ln \left(1 - F(Y_{N+1-i})\right) \right]$$

and F is the cumulative distribution function of the specified distribution. We can assess the results by looking at the resulting p value.

Figure 2.15 shows a normal distribution with a sample size of 27. The same data is shown in a histogram, probability plot, dot plot and a box blot.

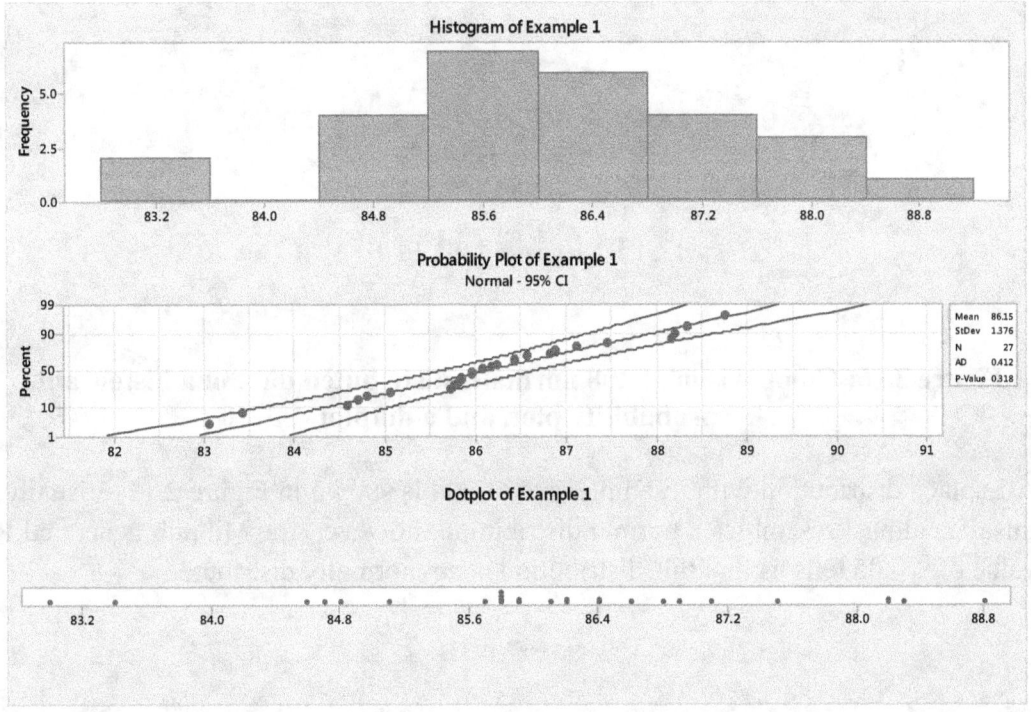

Figure 2.15: Comparison of 27 normally distributed data in a histogram, probability plot, and a dotplot

Figure 2.16 shows a normal distribution with sample a size of 208. Notice how the data is concentrated in the center of the histogram, probability plot, dot plot, and box plot.

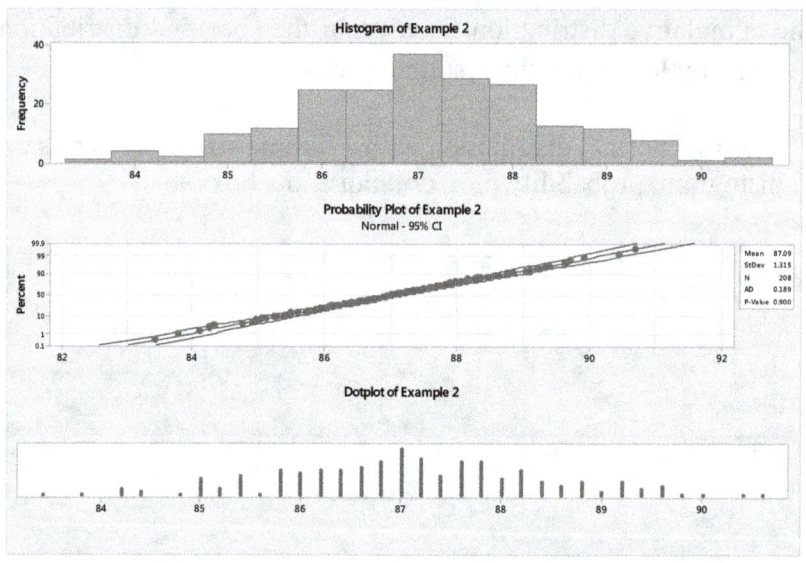

Figure 2.16: Comparison of 208 normally distributed data in a histogram, probability plot, and a dotplot

A Laplace distribution with a sample size of 208 is shown in Figure 2.17. Visually, this data almost resembles a normal distribution; however, the Minitab generated P value of < 0.05 tells us that this distribution is not normally distributed.

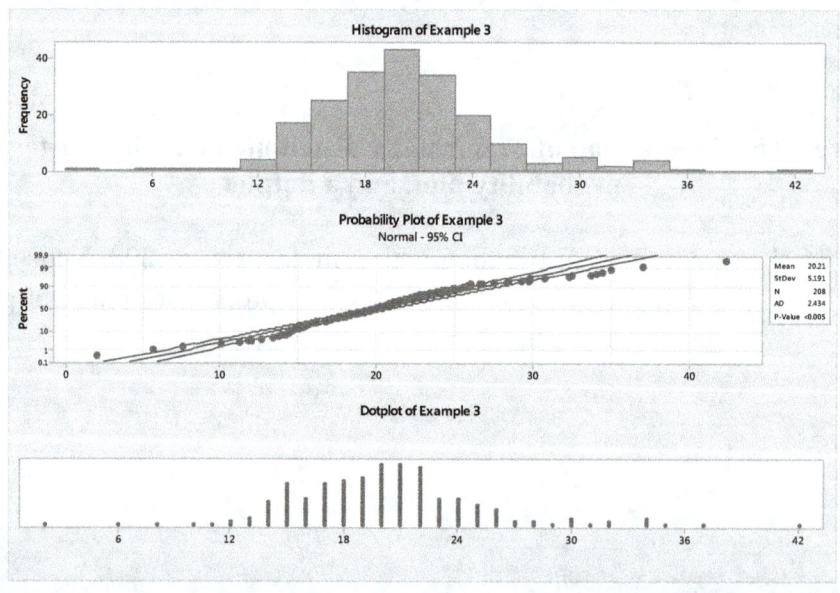

Figure 2.17: Comparison of 208 non-normally distributed data in a histogram, probability plot, and a dotplot

Figure 2.18 below shows a uniform distribution with a sample size of 270. Even without looking at the P value we can quickly see that the data is not normally distributed.

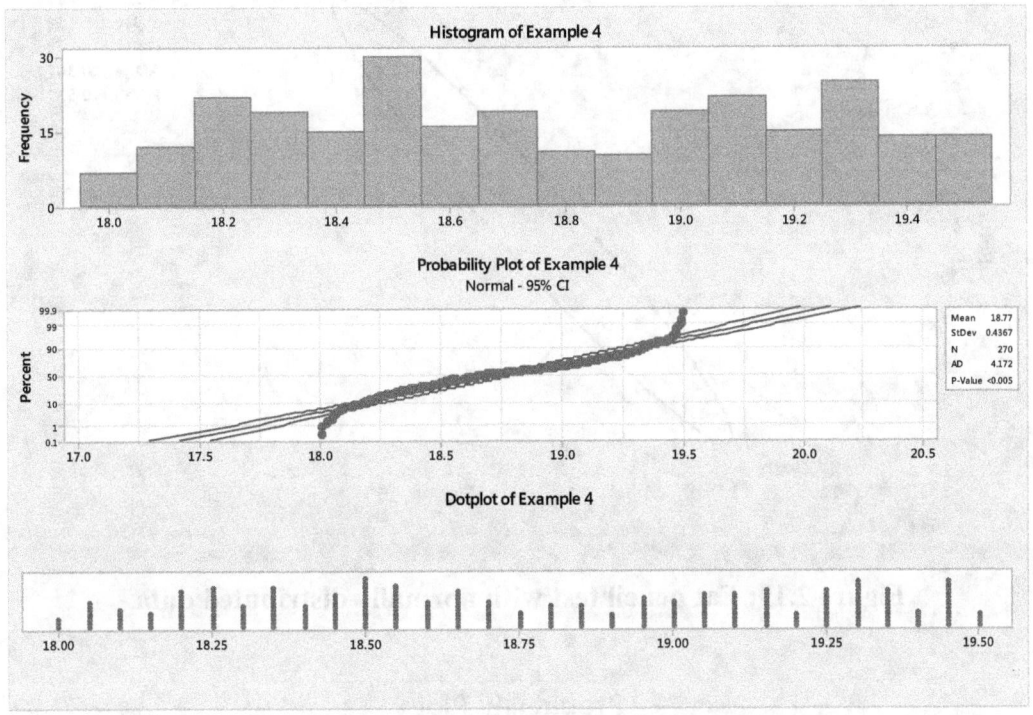

Figure 2.18: Comparison of 270 non-normally distributed data in a histogram, probability plot, and a dotplot

Back in the days of hand-drawn probability plots, the "fat pencil test" was often used to evaluate normality. The data was plotted and the distribution was considered normal if all of the data points could be covered by a thick pencil ah shown in Figure 2.19 and 2.20. The fat pencil test was quick and easy. Unfortunately, it is not as accurate as the Anderson-Darling test and is not a substitution for an actual test.

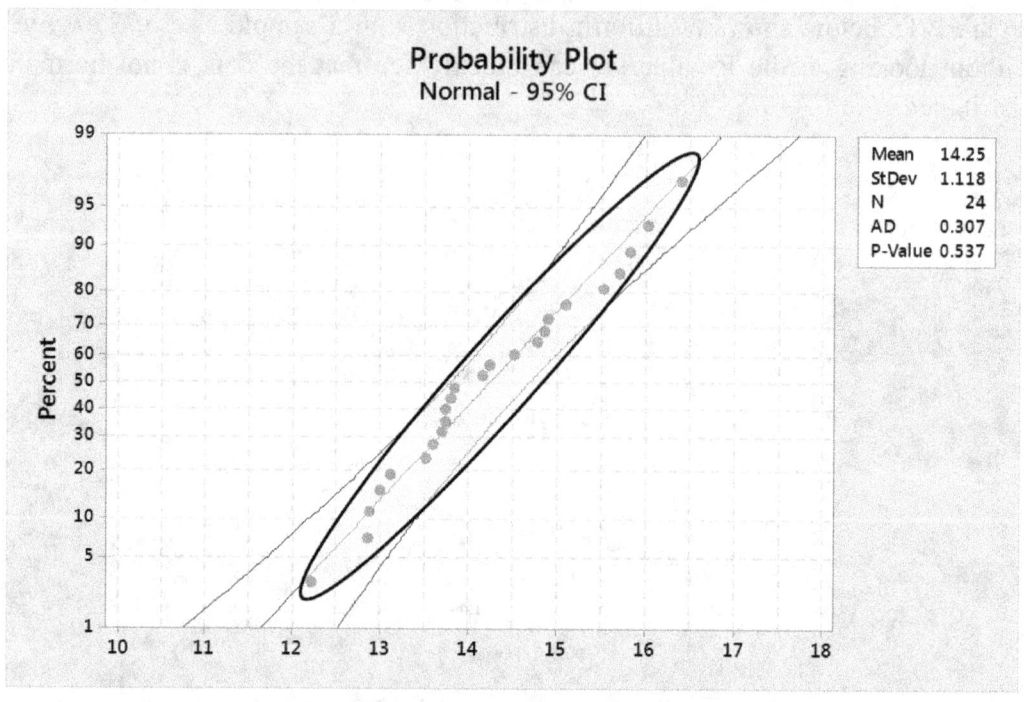

Figure 2.19: Fat pencil test with normally distributed data

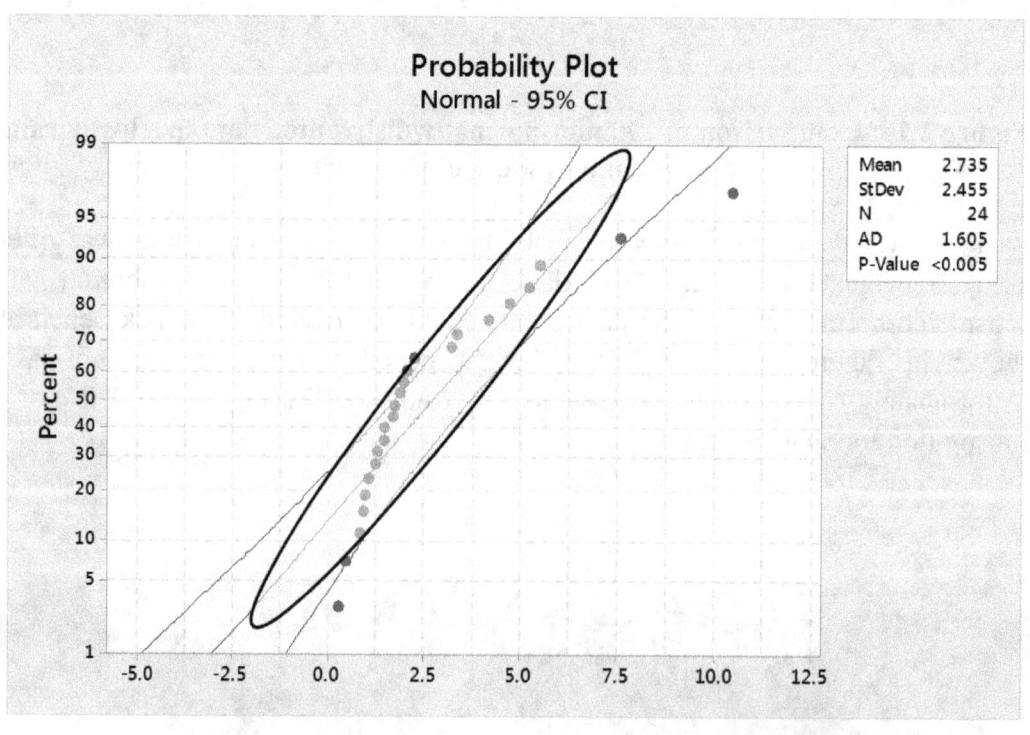

Figure 2.20: Fat pencil test with non-normally distributed data

IMPROVING PRODUCTS, SERVICES AND PROCESSES

The proper identification of a statistical distribution is critical for properly performing many types of hypothesis tests or for control charting as some methods require data to be normally distributed. Fortunately, we can now asses our data without having to rely on hand-drawn tests and a large diameter pencil.

To test for normality using the data in Table 2.12 to create a probability plot, go to the **Graph > Probability Plot** click on "Single." Then, enter the column containing the data. Minitab will generate a probability plot of your data as shown in Figure 2.21. Notice the P-value is 0.719. We would fail to reject the null hypothesis that the distribution of our data is equal to a normal distribution when we use a P-value of 0.05.

Data
26.93
25.18
26.62
25.95
27.05
26.01
25.17
27.46
26.21
25.93
28.09
26.08
25.74
27.28
25.08
26.14
25.78
24.84
26.6
27.08

Table 2.12: Data for a probability plot, histogram, and dotplot

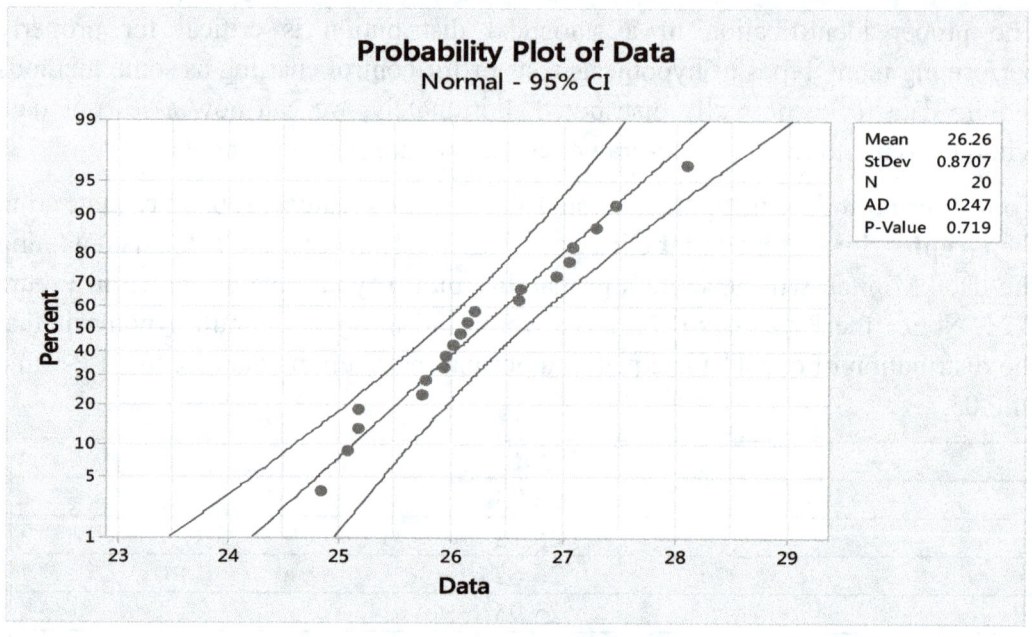

Figure 2.21: Probability plot

To create a histogram, go to **Graph > Histogram** and select "Simple" and select the column contain the data. The resulting histogram is shown in Figure 2.22.

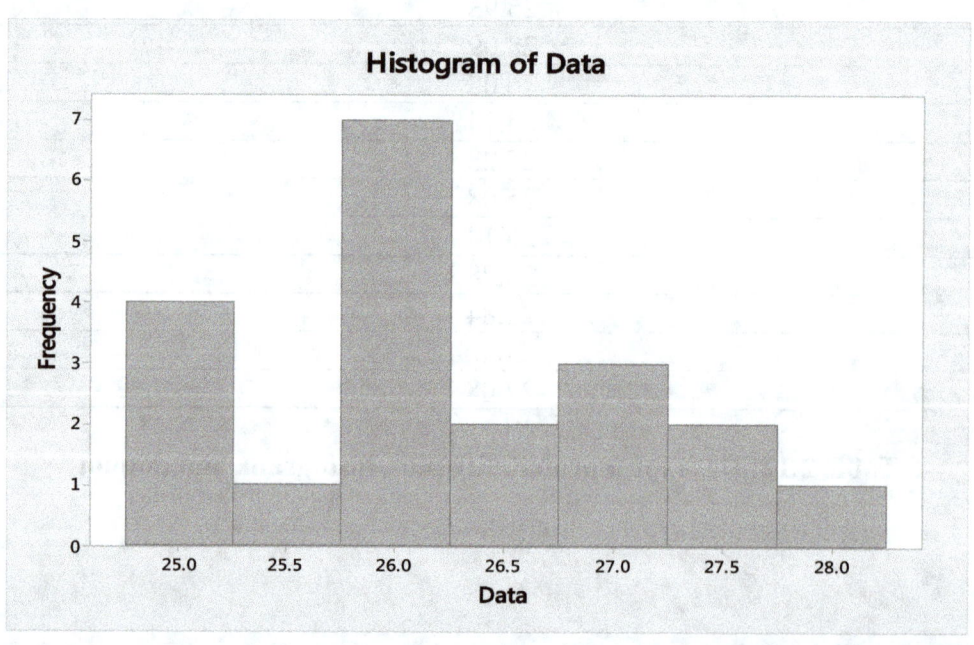

Figure 2.22: Histogram

To create a dotplot, go to **Graph > Dotplot** and **Select One Y > Simple** and then enter the data and Minitab creates the dotplot depicted in Figure 2.23.

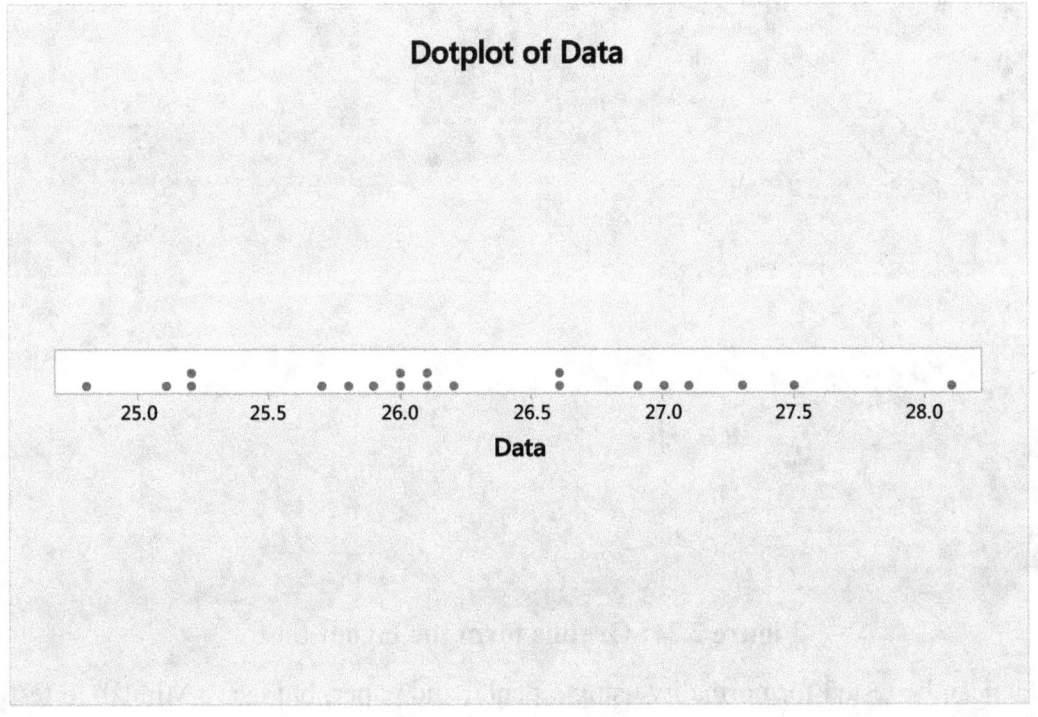

Figure 2.23: Dotplot

Previous examples have shown histograms probability plots, and dotplots combined into one graph. This can easily be done by clicking on any graph and then going to Editor > Layout Tool and selecting the desired graphs. Previous example used graphs in one column and that can be achieved by changing the number of rows and columns. The default version is shown below in Figure 2.24.

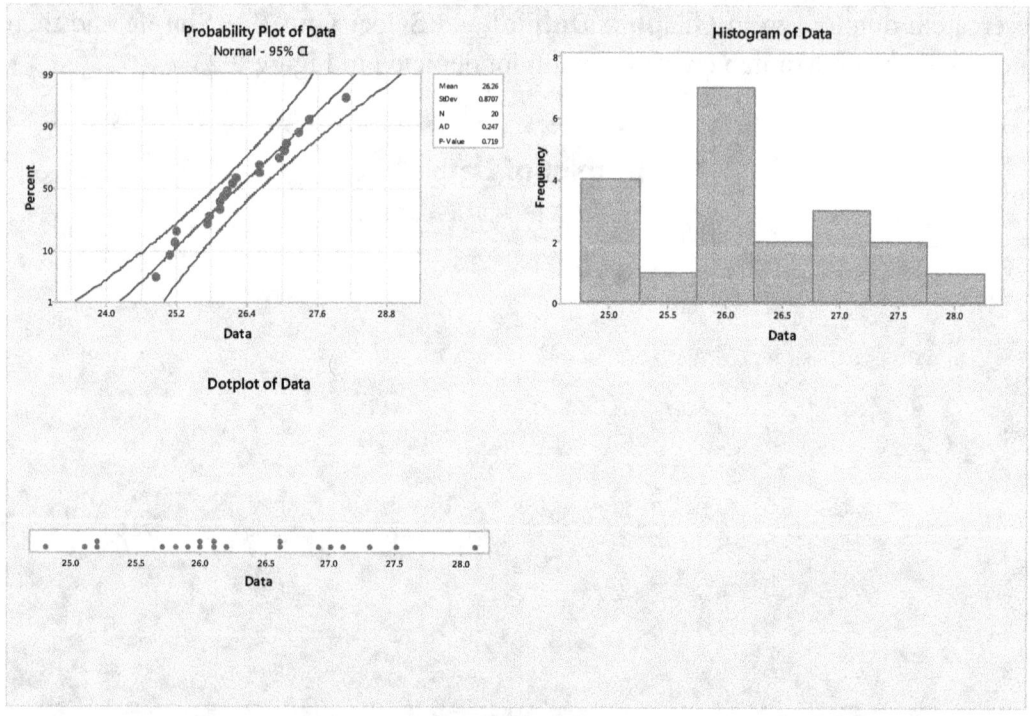

Figure 2.24: Graphs form the layout tool

Data can be tested for normality using a pencil and paper, but using Minitab to test data for normality is far more reliable than a fat pencil test and generally quicker and easier in addition to offering many ways to graphically depict the data. However, the fat pencil test may still be a viable option if you absolutely must analyze your data during a power outage.

CHAPTER 3

Hypothesis Testing

Chapter three begins with a discussion of hypothesis testing and P-values. Often, a P-value of 0.05 is used in hypothesis testing; however, the risk of an incorrect result increases as multiple tests are performed. The chapter then describes performing a two sample t-test using Minitab to test the means of two samples. The example also demonstrates creating an individual value plots and boxplots for simultaneously displaying multiple data sets.

Performing a two proportion test is also described. Here, an example based on a famous historical study is used to explain how to plan a statistical study and how to perform the actual test using Minitab. The concept of the gamblers fallacy is used to illustrate a test of two proportions. An unrealistic hypothetical example is then used to show a situation comparable to real-world industrial situations in which multiple statistical methods are required and statistics alone can't give the right answer; the person performing the study must make decisions. Another hypothetical example is then used to show how to perform an ANOVA to test multiple means.

3.1 Hypothesis Testing and P Values

Programs such as the Minitab Statistical Software make hypothesis testing easier; but no program can think for the experimenter. Anybody performing a statistical hypothesis test must understand what p values mean in regards to their statistical results as well as potential limitations of statistical hypothesis testing.

A p value of 0.05 is frequently used during statistical hypothesis testing. This p value indicates that if there is no effect (or if the null hypothesis is true), you'd obtain the observed difference or more in 5% of studies due to random sampling error. However, performing multiple hypothesis tests with p > 0.05 increases the chance of a false positive.

This is well illustrated by the online comic XKCD, which depicted somebody stating that jelly beans cause acne (see Figure 3.1) (XKCD 2017).

Figure 3.1: p-values comic. xkcd.com comic from http://xkcd.com/882/ used under Creative Commons Attribution- NonCommercial 2.5 License. http://xkcd.com/license.html

Scientists investigated and found no link, so the person made the claim that it is only a certain color jelly bean that caused acne. The scientists then test 20 different colors of jelly beans with p > 0.05. Only the green jelly bean had a p value less than 0.05.

The comic ends with a newspaper reporting a link between green jelly beans and acne. The newspaper points out there is 95% confidence with only a 5% chance of coincidence. What is wrong with the conclusion?

We can determine the chance that there will be no false conclusions by using the binomial formula.

$$P(0) = \frac{20!}{(20-0)!\,0!}(0.05)^0 * (0.95)^{20-0} = 0.358$$

This means that we have a 35.8% chance of performing 20 hypothesis tests without getting a false positive (or, as statisticians refer to it, the family error rate) when using an alpha level of 0.05. We can also calculate the probability that we have at least one incorrect result due to random chance.

$$P(\geq 1) = 1 - P(0) = 0.642$$

The chance that at least one result will be a false positive when performing 20 hypothesis tests using an alpha level of 0.05 is 64.2%.

So the press release in the XKCD comic may have been a bit premature.

Suppose I had 14 samples with a mean of 87.2 and I wanted to know if the mean is actually 85.2. The data is shown in Table 3.1.

Data
81.11
91.46
86.87
86.6
89.19
89.59
84.67
86.71
83.97
90.59
88.4
88.71
85.19
83.7

Table 3.1: Data

I performed a One-Sample T-test using Minitab by going to **Stat > Basic Statistics > 1 Sample t** and I entered the summarized data. I checked the "Perform hypothesis test box" and then selected "Options" and used the default confidence level of 95.0. This corresponds to an alpha of 0.05. The resulting session window is shown in Figure 3.2.

One-Sample T: Data

Descriptive Statistics

N	Mean	StDev	SE Mean	95% CI for µ
14	86.911	2.945	0.787	(85.211; 88.612)

µ: mean of Data

Test

Null hypothesis $H_0: \mu = 85.2$
Alternative hypothesis $H_1: \mu \neq 85.2$

T-Value	P-Value
2.17	0.049

Figure 3.2: Minitab session window for a One-Sample T-Test

I performed the test and the resulting p value was 0.049, which is close to but still below 0.05, so I can reject my null hypothesis. If I performed the test repeatedly, as in the XKCD example, I might have failed to reject the null hypothesis, because the 5% probability adds up with additional tests.

There are alternatives to statistical hypothesis testing (Ziliak and McCloskey 2012); for example, Bayesian inference could be used in place of hypothesis testing with p values. But alternative methods have their own weaknesses, and they may be difficult for non-statisticians to use.

Instead of avoiding the use of hypothesis testing, we should account for its limitations. For example, by realizing that each repeat of the test increases the chance of a false positive, as illustrated by XKCD's jelly bean example.

We can't simply retest over and over using the same p value and then conclude that we have results with statistical significance. For situations such as in the XKCD example, Simons, Nelson and Simonsohn recommend disclosing the total number of tests that were performed (2011). Had we known that 20 tests had been performed with p > 0.05 we could realize that we may not need to avoid green jellybeans after all.

3.2 A Minitab Holiday Tale: Featuring the Two Sample t-Test

Aaron and Billy are two very competitive—and not always well-behaved—eight-year-old twin brothers. They constantly strive to outdo each other, no matter what the subject. If the boys are given a piece of pie for dessert, they each automatically want to make sure that their own piece of pie is bigger than the other's piece of pie. This causes much exasperation, aggravation and annoyance for their parents. Especially when it happens in a restaurant (although the restaurant situation has improved, since they have been asked not to return to most local restaurants).

Sending the boys to their rooms never helped. The two would just compete to see who could stay in their room longer. This Christmas their parents were at wits' ends, and they decided the boys needed to be taught a lesson so they could grow up to be upstanding citizens. Instead of the new bicycles the boys were going to get—and probably just race till they crashed anyway—their parents decided to give them each a bag of coal.

An astute reader might ask, "But what does this have to do with Minitab?" Well, dear reader, the boys need to figure out who got the most coal. Immediately upon opening their packages, the boys carefully weighed each piece of coal and entered the data (see Table 3.2) into Minitab.

Aaron	Billy
6.9	7.5
8.8	7
6.6	7.5
8.8	8.8
6.7	8.7
8.3	8.8
7.0	8.5
7.1	9.3
10.4	5.7
6.7	6.9
7.1	7.8
7.7	6.7
9.6	8.7
7.9	8.6
5.2	7.3
8.7	8.8
6.6	9.6
7.1	6.8
7.6	9.1
8.5	6.9
6.5	7.6
7.8	8.8
6.8	7.6
9.2	8.8

IMPROVING PRODUCTS, SERVICES AND PROCESSES

8	7.9
6.7	7.8
10.1	7.4
6.7	5.7
8.0	8.1
7.7	7.7
9.5	9.8
8.4	7.4
8.1	8.4
7.9	9.8
8.4	7.4

Table 3.2: The weight of coal for Aaron and Billy

Then they selected **Stat > Basic Statistics > Display Descriptive Statistics** and used the "Statistics" options dialog to select the items they wanted, including the sum of the weights they'd entered. The resulting session window is shown in Figure 3.3.

Descriptive Statistics: Aaron; Billy

Statistics

Variable	N	N*	Mean	SE Mean	StDev	Minimum	Q1	Median	Q3	Maximum
Aaron	35	0	7.797	0.195	1.151	5.184	6.757	7.795	8.532	10.432
Billy	35	0	7.982	0.174	1.032	5.697	7.363	7.776	8.800	9.789

Figure 3.3: Session window for descriptive statistics

Billy quickly saw that he had the most coal, and yelled, "I have 279.383 ounces and you only have 272.896 ounces, and the mean of my pieces of coal is more than the mean of yours. Mine weigh more, so our parents must love me more."

"Not so fast," said Aaron. "You may have a higher mean value, but is the difference statistically significant?" There was only one thing left for the boys to do: perform a two sample t-test. A two sample t-test is used to determine if there is a statistically significant difference between two means (Lawson and Erjavec 2001).

In Minitab, Aaron selected **Stat > Basic Statistics > 2-Sample t** and then selected "Each sample in its own column" and entered the columns containing the data.

The boys left the default values at a confidence level of 95.0 and a hypothesized difference of 0. The alternative hypothesis was "Difference ≠ hypothesized difference" because the only question they were asking was "Is there a statistically significant difference?" between the two data sets.

The two troublemakers also selected "Graphs" and checked the options to display an individual value plot and a boxplot. They knew they should look at their data. Having the graphs available would also make it easier for them to communicate their results to higher authorities, in this case, their poor parents.

Both the individual value plots in Figure 3.4) and boxplots in Figure 3.5 showed that Aaron's bag of coal had pieces with the highest individual weights. But he also had the pieces with the least weight. So the values for his Christmas coal were scattered across a wider range than the values for Billy's Christmas coal. But was there really a difference?

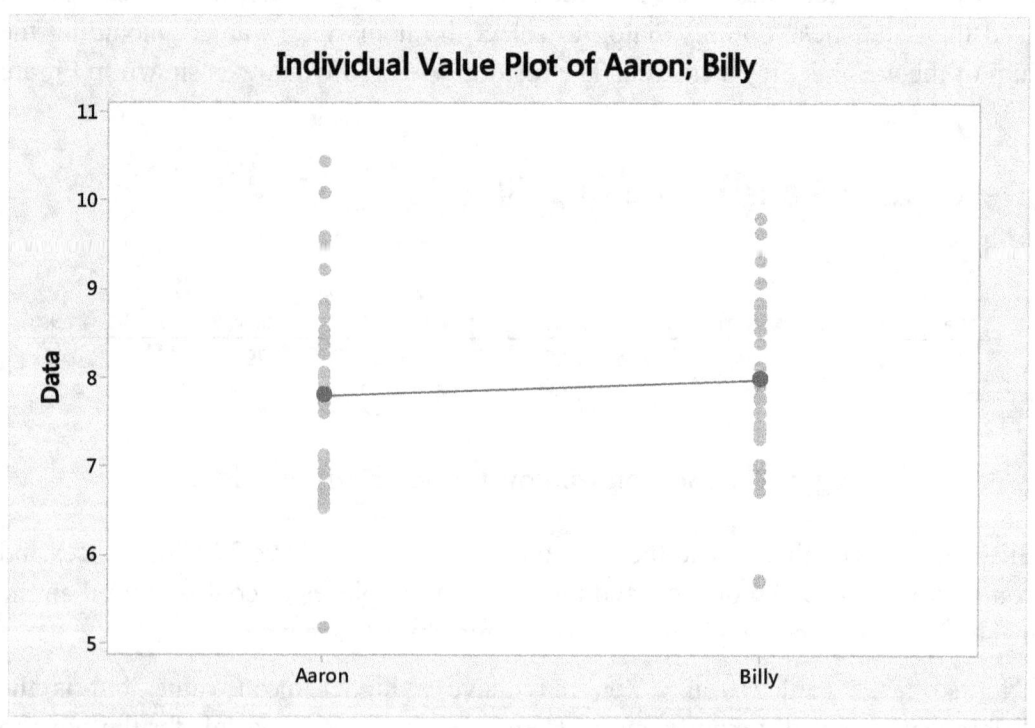

Figure 3.4: Individual value plots

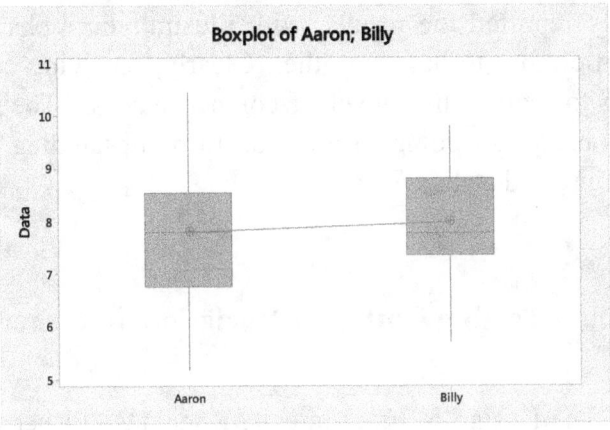

Figure 3.5: Boxplots

Billy went running for his tables of Student's t-scores so he could interpret the resulting t-value of -0.71. Aaron simply looked at the resulting p-value of 0.481 in the Minitab session widow as shown in Figure 3.6. The p-value was greater than 0.05 so the boys could not conclude there was a difference in the means of the weights of their Christmas "presents."

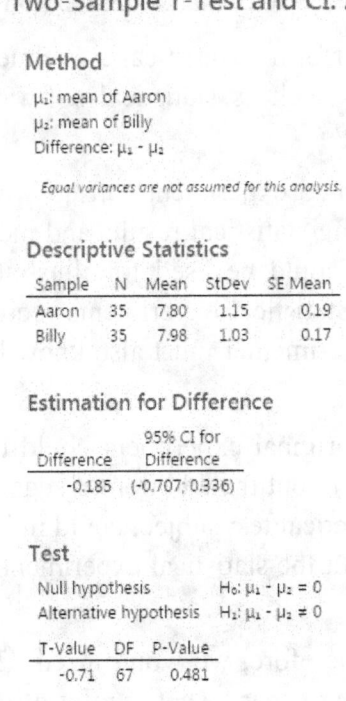

Figure 3.6: Minitab session window for Two-Sample T-Test

The boys dutifully reported the results, with illustrative graphs, each demanding that they get a little more to best the other. Clearly, receiving coal for Christmas had done nothing to reduce their level of competitiveness. Their parents realized the boys were probably not going to grow up to be upstanding citizens, but they may at least become good statisticians.

Happy Holidays.

3.3 The Gentleman Tasting Coffee: A Variation on Fisher's Famous Experiment

In the 1935 book The Design of Experiments, Ronald A. Fisher used the example of a lady tasting tea to demonstrate basic principles of statistical experiments. In Fisher's example, a lady made the claim that she could taste whether milk or tea was poured first into her cup, so Fisher did what any good statistician would do—he performed an experiment (1971).

The lady in question, Dr. Muriel Bristol, was given eight random combinations of cups of tea with either the tea poured first or the milk poured first. She was required to divide the cups into two groups based on whether the milk or tea was poured in first. Fisher's presentation of the experiment was not about the tasting of tea; rather, it was a method to explain the proper use of statistical methods.

Understanding how to properly perform a statistical experiment is critical, whether you're using a data analysis tool such as statistical software or performing the calculations by hand.

The Experiment A poorly performed experiment can do worse than just provide bad data; it could lead to misleading statistical results and incorrect conclusions. A variation on Fisher's experiment could be used for illustrating how to properly perform a statistical experiment. Statistical experiments require more than just an understanding of statistics. An experimenter must also know how to plan and carry out an experiment.

A possible variation on Fisher's original experiment could be performed using a man tasting coffee made with or without the addition of sugar. The objective is not actually to determine if the hypothetical test subject could indeed determine if there is sugar in the coffee, but to present the statistical experiment in a way that is both practical and easy to understand.

We decide to perform 44 trials; therefore, we would need 22 cups of coffee with sugar and 22 cups of coffee without sugar. That is a lot of coffee so the cup size will be 10 ml each. There is a risk that different pots of coffee will not be the same as each other due to differences such as the amount of coffee grain used or the cooling of the coffee over time. To counter this, the experimenter would brew one large pot of coffee and then separate it into two containers; one container would receive the sugar.

A table is then created to plan the experiment and record the results. The first 22 samples would contain sugar and the next 22 would not. Simply providing the test subject with the cups in the order they are listed would risk the subject realizing the sugar is in the first half so randomization will be required to ensure the test subject is unaware of which cups contain sugar. Fisher referred to randomization as an "essential safeguard" (1971). A random integer generator can used to assign the run order to the samples.

The accuracy of the results could be increased by using blinding. The experimenter may subconsciously give the test subject signals that could indicate the actual condition of the coffee. This could be avoided by having the cups of coffee delivered by a second person who is unaware of the status of the cups. The use of blinding adds an additional layer of protection to the experiment.

Figure 3.7 contains the data collection sheet; however, the first half of the experiment is with sugar and the second half is without. It is possible that somebody may notice the sudden change so the test order should be randomized. Right click on column C3-T and select "Insert columns." Go to Calc > Random Data > Integer and enter 44as the number of rows to generate. Store the results in Randomized order and list 1 as "Minimum value" and 44 as the "Maximum value."

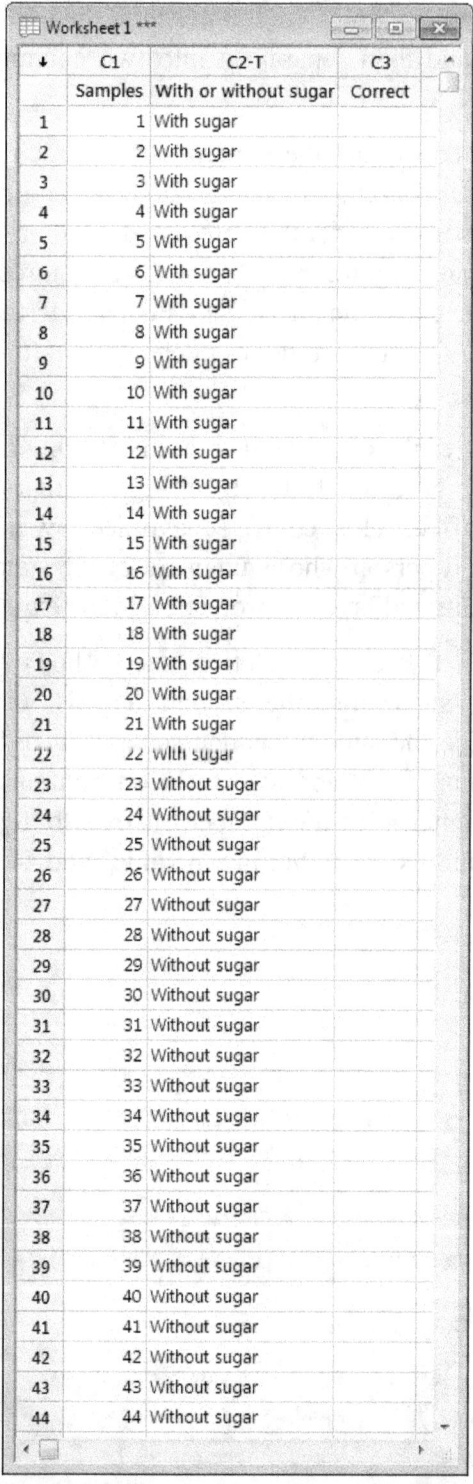

Figure 3.7: Minitab worksheet for data collection

IMPROVING PRODUCTS, SERVICES AND PROCESSES

Next, the order needs to be randomized so go to Data > Sort and Enter Randomized order in "Columns to sort by." Change "Storage location for the sorted columns" to "In the original columns." For "Columns to sort," select the samles, randomized order and with or without sugar.

The Analysis Suppose the test subject correctly identified 38 out of 44 samples, which results in a proportion of 38/44 or 0.86. This could have been the result of random chance and not actually correctly identifying the samples so a one sample proportion test could be used to evaluate the results. We can perform the analysis using statistical software; however, we can either use summarized data or we can enter the date in Table 3.3 into Minitab.

Samples	Randomized order	With or without sugar	Correct
1	1	With sugar	Yes
2	2	With sugar	Yes
23	3	Without sugar	Yes
3	4	With sugar	Yes
24	5	Without sugar	Yes
4	6	With sugar	No
5	7	With sugar	Yes
25	8	Without sugar	Yes
26	9	Without sugar	Yes
27	10	Without sugar	Yes
6	11	With sugar	Yes
28	12	Without sugar	Yes
7	13	With sugar	Yes
8	14	With sugar	No
29	15	Without sugar	Yes
9	16	With sugar	No
10	17	With sugar	Yes
30	18	Without sugar	Yes
31	19	Without sugar	Yes
32	20	Without sugar	Yes
11	21	With sugar	No
12	22	With sugar	Yes
33	23	Without sugar	Yes
13	24	With sugar	Yes
34	25	Without sugar	Yes
35	26	Without sugar	No
36	27	Without sugar	Yes
14	28	With sugar	Yes

37	29	Without sugar	Yes
15	30	With sugar	Yes
16	31	With sugar	Yes
38	32	Without sugar	Yes
17	33	With sugar	Yes
18	34	With sugar	Yes
39	35	Without sugar	Yes
40	36	Without sugar	Yes
19	37	With sugar	Yes
20	38	With sugar	Yes
41	39	Without sugar	Yes
42	40	Without sugar	Yes
43	41	Without sugar	Yes
21	42	With sugar	No
22	43	With sugar	Yes
44	44	Without sugar	Yes

Table 3.3: The results of the experiment

To use summarized data in Minitab, select **Stat > Basic Statistics > 1 Proportion** and enter 38 and the "Number of events" and 44 as the "Number of trials." Select "Perform hypothesis test," enter 0.5 as the "Hypothesized proportion" and then click on "Options." Under "Method," select "Normal approximation." The Minitab default setting is the exact method; however, the normal approximation is what we used when we did the calculations by hand. The Minitab results are shown in Figure 3.8.

Test and CI for One Proportion

Method

p: event proportion
Normal approximation method is used for this analysis.

Descriptive Statistics

N	Event	Sample p	95% CI for p
44	38	0.863636	(0.762237; 0.965036)

Test

Null hypothesis H_0: p = 0.5
Alternative hypothesis H_1: p ≠ 0.5

Z-Value	P-Value
4.82	0.000

Figure 3.8: Session window for One Proportion test using summarized data

Minitab gives us a p-value, which in this case is 0.00 And as a wise statistician once said, "If the P-value's low, the null must go."

The same analysis could be performed using data in the Minitab worksheet. Go to Stat > **Basic Statistics** > **1 Proportion** and select "One or more samples, each in a column" from the dropdown menu. Then select the column containing the data and again click on "Options." Under "Method," select "Normal approximation." The new Minitab results are shown in Figure 3.9.

```
Test and CI for One Proportion: Correct

Method
Event: Correct = Yes
p: proportion where Correct = Yes
Normal approximation method is used for this analysis.

Descriptive Statistics
 N   Event   Sample p    95% CI for p
44     38    0.863636   (0.762237; 0.965036)

Test
Null hypothesis          H₀: p = 0.5
Alternative hypothesis   H₁: p ≠ 0.5

Z-Value   P-Value
 4.82      0.000
```

Figure 3.9: Session window for One Proportion test using actual data

It is important to note that rejecting the null hypothesis does not automatically mean we accept the alternative hypothesis. Accepting the alternative hypothesis is a strong conclusion; we can only conclude there is insufficient evidence to reject it when compared against the null hypothesis and the null hypothesis only used as a comparison with the alternative hypothesis. Fisher himself, in *The Design of Experiments,* tells us "the null hypothesis is never proved or established, but is possibly disproved, in the course of experimentation" (1971).

Fisher's Results As for the original experiment, Fisher's son-in-law the statistician George E.P. Box informs us in the lady in question was Dr. Muriel Bristol and her future husband reported she got almost all choices correct (1976). Salsburg also confirms the lady in question could indeed taste the difference; he was so informed by Professor Hugh Smith, who was present while the lady tasted her tea (2001).

Fisher never actually reported the results; however, what mattered in Fisher's tale is not whether or not somebody could taste a difference in a drink, but using the proper methodology when performing a statistical experiment.

3.4 Birds Versus Statisticians: Testing the Gambler's Fallacy

The statistician Joel Smith posted a blog about an incident in which he was pooped on by a bird. Twice (2015). I suspect many people would assume the odds of it happening twice are very low, so they would incorrectly assume they are safer after such a rare event happens.

I don't have data on how often birds poop on one person, and I assume Joel is unwilling to stand under a flock of berry-fed birds waiting to collect data for me, so I'll simply make up some numbers for illustration purposes only.

Suppose there is a 5% chance of being pooped on by a bird during a vacation. That means the probability of being pooped on is 0.05. The probability of being pooped on twice during the vacation is 0.0025 (0.05 x 0.05) or 0.25%, and the probability of being pooped on three times is 0.000125 (0.05. x 0.05 x 0.05).

Joel has already been pooped on twice. So, what is the probability of our intrepid statistician being pooped on a *third* time?

The probability is 0.05. If you said 0.000125, then you may have made a mistake known as the Gambler's Fallacy or the Monte Carlo Fallacy. This fallacy is named after the mistaken belief that things will average out in the short-term. A gambler who has suffered repeated losses may incorrectly assume that the recent losses mean a win is due soon (Mlodinow 2008). Things *will* balance out in the long term, but the odds do not reset after each event. Joel could correctly conclude the probability of a bird pooping on him during his vacation are low and the odds of being pooped on twice are much lower. But being pooped on one time does not affect the probability of it happening a second time.

There is a caveat here. The probabilities only apply if the meeting of poop and Joel are random events. Perhaps birds, for reasons understood only by birds, have an inordinate fondness for Joel. Our probability calculations would no longer apply in such a situation. This would be like calculating the probabilities of a coin toss when there is some characteristic that causes the coin to land more on one side than on the other.

We can perform an experiment to determine if Joel is just a victim of the odds or if there is something that makes the birds target him. The generally low occurrence rate would make it difficult to collect data in a reasonable amount of time so we should perform an experiment to collect data. We could send Joel to a bird

IMPROVING PRODUCTS, SERVICES AND PROCESSES

sanctuary for two weeks and record the number of times he is pooped on. Somebody of approximately the same size and appearance as Joel could be used as a control. Both Joel and the control should be dressed the same to ensure that birds are not targeting a particular color or clothing brand. Table 3.4 shows the hypothetical results of our little experiment.

Day	Joel	Control	Day
1	13	8	1
2	8	6	2
3	11	7	3
4	4	8	4
5	6	5	5
6	9	9	6
7	12	2	7
8	6	2	8
9	6	5	9
10	5	6	10
11	7	6	11
12	3	1	12
13	4	6	13
14	5	9	14

Table 3.4: Results of the experiment

We can see that Joel was hit 99 times, while the control was only hit 80 times. But does this difference mean anything? To find out, we can determine if there is a statistically significant difference between the number of times Joel was hit and the number of times the control was hit. We can use the Poisson distribution for evaluating the occurrence of events within a given interval (Vinning and Kowalski 2006).

Enter the data into Minitab and then go to **Stat > Basic Statistics > 2-Sample Poisson Rate** and select "Each sample is in its own column." Go to "Options" and select "Difference > hypothesized difference" as the alternative hypothesis for a one-tailed upper tailed test. The resulting Minitab session windows (see Fig. 3.10) shows two P-values; one for the Exact method and one for the Normal approximation. Both are greater than the alpha of 0.05 so we fail to reject the null hypothesis. Although there was a higher occurrence rate for Joel, we have no reason to think that birds are especially attracted to him.

```
Test and CI for Two-Sample Poisson Rates: Joel; Control

Method
λ₁: Poisson rate of Joel
λ₂: Poisson rate of Control
Difference: λ₁ - λ₂

Descriptive Statistics
                    Total
Sample    N    Occurrences    Sample Rate
Joel      14       99           7.07143
Control   14       80           5.71429

Estimation for Difference
                 95% Lower
Estimated        Bound for
Difference       Difference
1.35714          -0.214760

Test
Null hypothesis           H₀: λ₁ - λ₂ = 0
Alternative hypothesis    H₁: λ₁ - λ₂ > 0

Method                  Z-Value    P-Value
Exact                              0.089
Normal approximation    1.42       0.078
```

Figure 3.10: Minitab session window for Two-Sample Poisson Rates

Joel is well aware of the Gambler's Fallacy, so we can be assured that he is not under a false sense of security. He must know the probability of him getting struck a third time has not changed. But has he considered that these may not be random events? The experiment described here was only hypothetical. Perhaps Joel should consider wearing a sou'wester and rain coat the next time he takes a vacation in the sun.

3.5 Statistics: Another Weapon in the Galactic Patrol's Arsenal

E. E. Doc Smith, one of the greatest authors ever, wrote many classic books such as The Skylark of Space (Smith 1966a) and his Lensman series (Smith 1966b). Doc Smith's imagination knew no limits; his Galactic Patrol had millions of combat fleets under its command and possessed planets turned into movable, armored weapons platforms. Some of the Galactic Patrol's weapons may be well known. For example, there is the sunbeam, which concentrated the entire output of a sun's energy into one beam.

The Galactic Patrol also created the negasphere, a planet-sized dark matter/dark energy bomb that could eat through anything. I'll go out on a limb and assume that they first created a container that could contain such a substance, at least briefly.

When I read about such technology, I always have to wonder "How did they test it?" I can see where Minitab Statistical Software could be very helpful to the

Galactic Patrol. How could the Galactic Patrol evaluate smaller, torpedo-sized units of negasphere? Suppose negasphere was created at the time of firing in a space torpedo and needed to be contained for the first 30 seconds after being fired, lest it break containment early and damage the ship that is firing it or rupture the torpedo before it reaches a space pirate.

Table 3.5 shows data collected from fifteen samples each of two materials that could be used for negasphere containment. Material 1 has a mean containment time of 33.951 seconds and Material 2 has a mean of 32.018 seconds. But is this difference statically significant? Does it even matter?

Material 1	Material 2
34.5207	32.1227
33.0061	31.9836
32.9733	31.9975
32.4381	31.9997
34.1364	31.9414
36.1568	32.0403
34.6487	32.1153
36.6436	31.9661
35.3177	32.067
32.4043	31.961
31.3107	32.0303
34.0913	32.0146
33.204	31.9865
32.5601	32.0079
35.8556	32.0328

Table 3.5: Material 1 and 2

The questions we're asking and the type and distribution of the data we have should determine the types of statistical test we perform. Many statistical tests for continuous data require an assumption of normality, and this can easily be tested in our statistical software by going to **Graphs > Probability Plot** and entering the columns containing the data. The resulting probability plots are shown in Figures 3.11 and 3.12

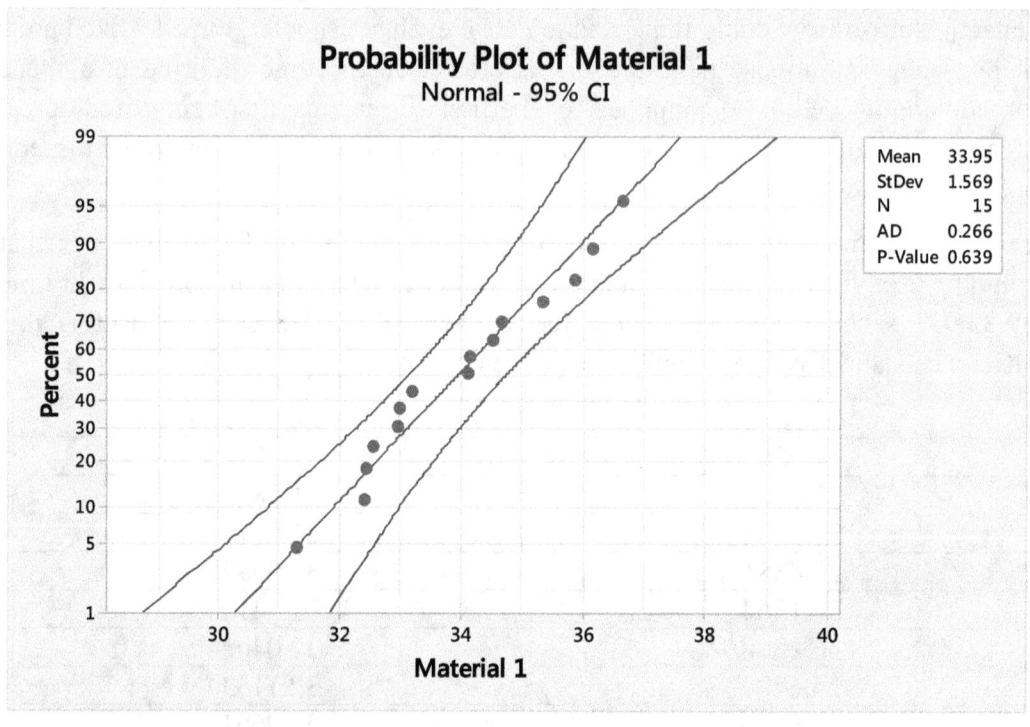

Figure 3.11: Probability plot for Material 1

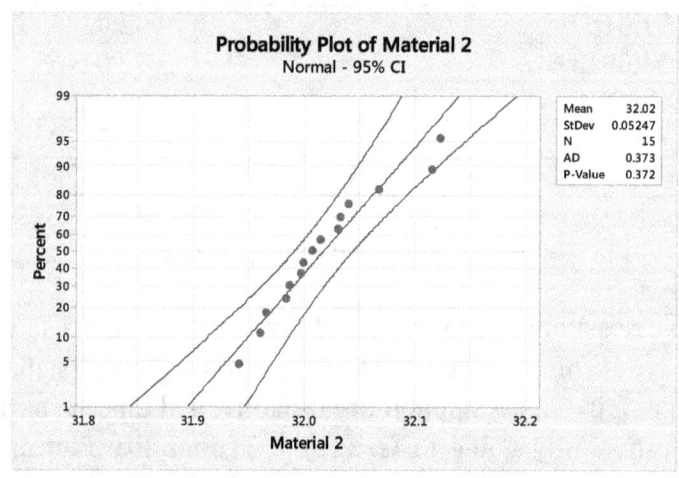

Figure 3.12: Probability plot for Material 2

The null hypothesis is "the data are normally distributed," and the resulting P-values are greater 0.05, so we fail to reject the null hypothesis. That means we can evaluate the data using tests that require the data to be normally distributed.

To determine if the mean of Material 1 is indeed greater than the mean of Material 2, we perform a two sample t-test: go to **Stat > Basic Statistics > 2 Sample t** and select "Each sample in its own column." We then choose "Options" and select "Difference > hypothesized difference." The resulting session window is shown in Figure 3.13.

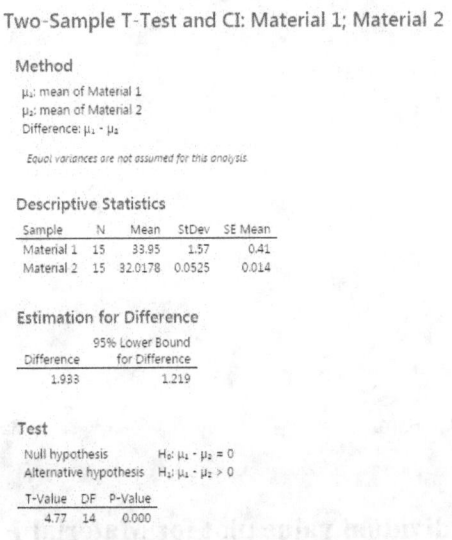

Figure 3.13: Session window for a Two-Sample T-Test

The P-value for the two sample t-test is less than 0.05, so we can conclude there is a statistically significant difference between the materials. But the two sample t-test does not give us a complete picture of the situation, so we should look at the data by going to **Graph > Individual Value Plot** and selecting **Simple graph > Multiple Y's** (see Fig. 3.14).

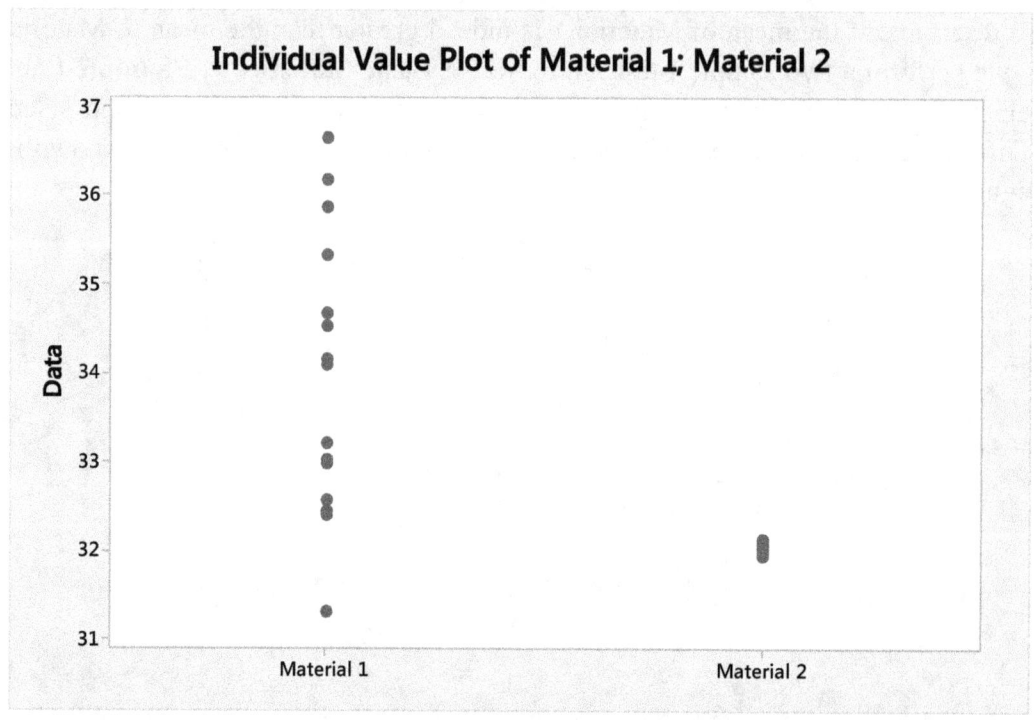

Figure 3.14: Individual value plot for Material 1 and Material 2

The mean of Material 1 may be higher, but our biggest concern is identifying a material that does not fail in 30 seconds or less. Material 2 appears to have far less variation and we can assess this by performing an F-test (Stephens 2004): go to **Stat > Basic Statistics > 2 Variances** and select "Each sample in its own column." Then choose "Options" and select "Ratio > hypothesized ratio." The data is normally distributed, so put a checkmark next to "Use test and confidence intervals based on normal distribution." The session window is shown in Figure 3.15 and the test and confidence interval is shown in Figure 3.16.

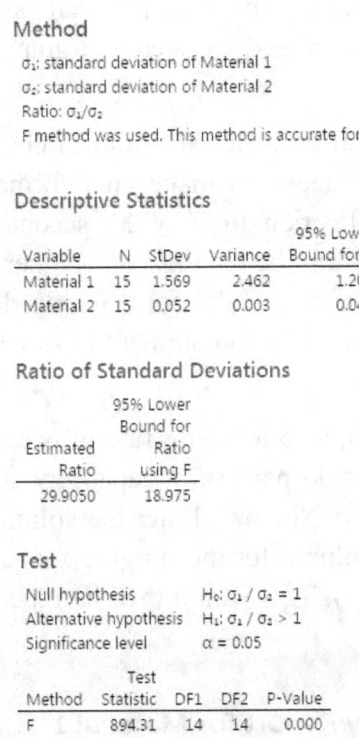

Figure 3.15: Session window for a Test of Two Variances

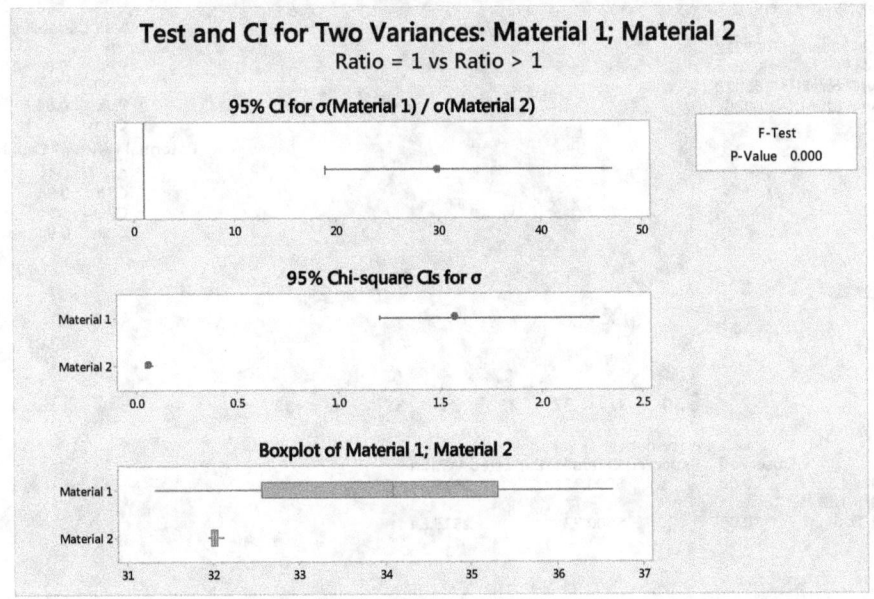

Figure 3.16: Graph for a Test of Two Variances

The P-value is less than 0.05, so we can conclude the evidence does supports the alternative hypothesis that the variance of the first material is greater than the variance of the second material. Having already looked at a graph of the data, this should come as no surprise

No statistical software program can tell us which material to choose, but Minitab can provide us with the information needed to make an informed decision. The objective is to exceed a lower specification limit of 30 seconds and the lower variability of Material 2 will achieve this better than the higher mean value for Material 1. Material 2 looks good, but the penalty for a wrong decision could be lost space ships if the negasphere breaches its containment too soon, so we must be certain.

The Galactic Patrol has millions of ships so a failure rate of even one per million would be unacceptably high so we should perform a capability study by going to **Quality Tools > Capability Analysis > Normal**. Enter the column containing the data for Material 1 and use the same column for the subgroup size and then enter a lower specification of 30 (see Fig. 3.17). This would then be repeated for Material 2 (see Fig. 3.18).

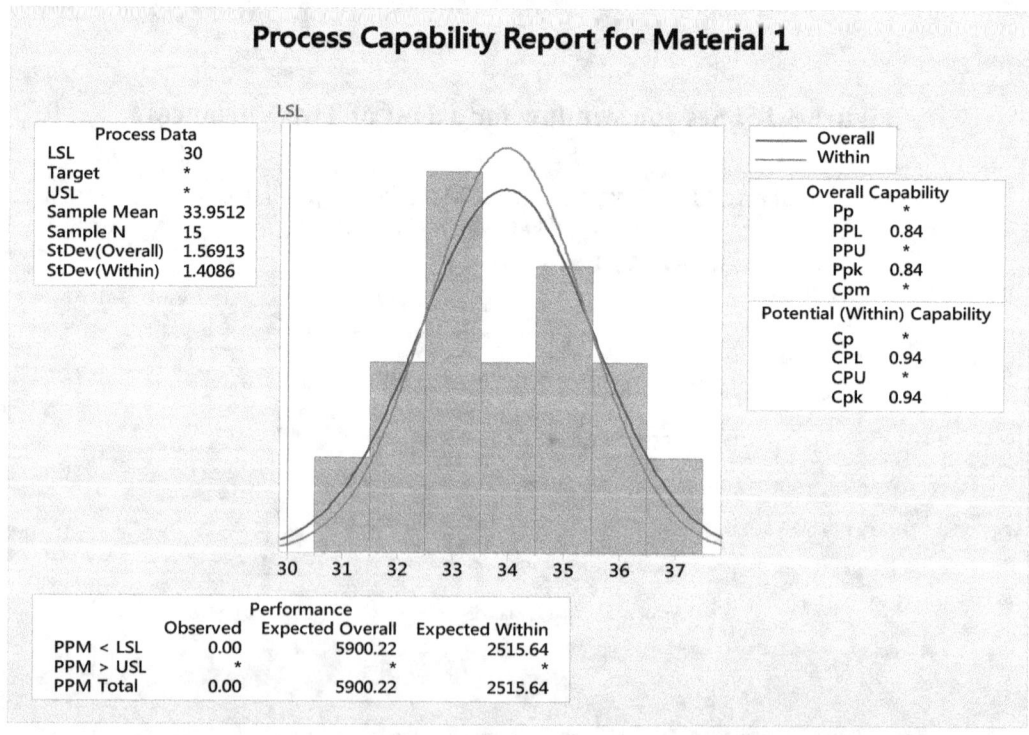

Figure 3.17: Capability report for Material 1

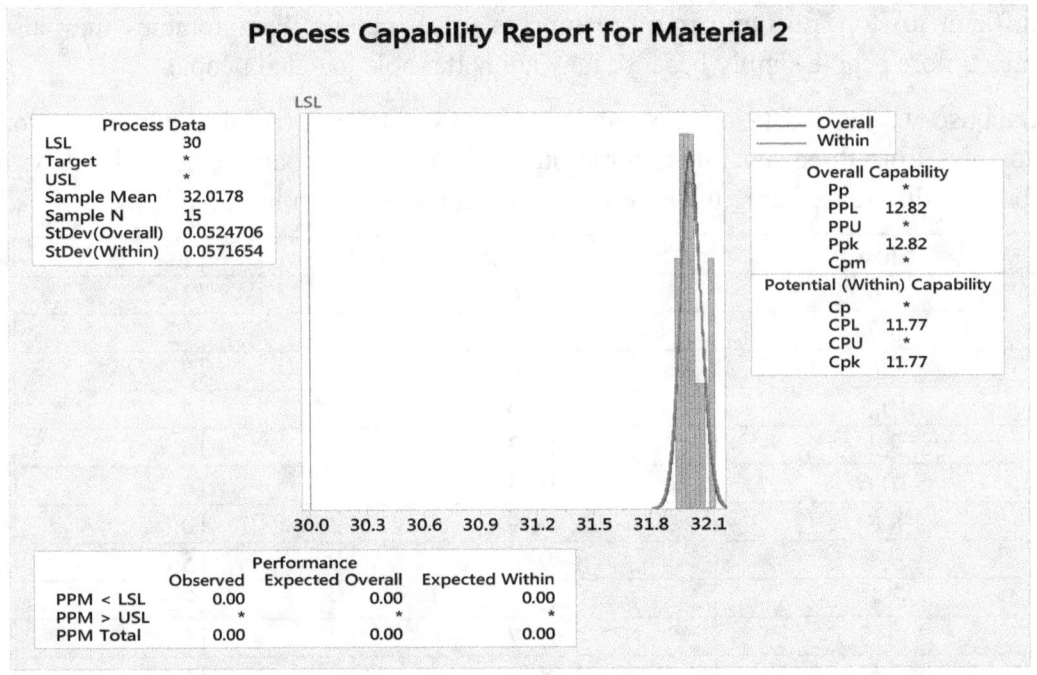

Figure 3.18: Capability report for Material 2

The sample size of 30 was low for a capability study; there should be at least 100 values. However, in spite of the low sample size, looking at the Minitab generated capability studies, we can see that Material 1 can be expected to fail thousands of times per million uses while Material 2 would is not expected to fail at all. In spite of the higher mean, the Galactic Patrol should use Material 2 for the negasephere torpedoes.

3.6 ANOVA and the Zombie Apocalypse

Zombies have been showing up in the news with actual researchers studying hypothetical zombie outbreaks (Dhar 2013). The mathematical modeling of a fictional zombie outbreak is relevant to actual disease outbreaks and it is probably more interesting to many readers than a paper on reproduction thresholds in modeling infectious diseases (Heathcote 2000). I won't criticize anybody who uses zombies as a ploy to attract readers as I am about to do the same here.

Mathematical models on zombie outbreaks may incorrect be if the researchers fail to consider the speed at which zombies move. Consider the slow and lumbering zombies of the classic film *Night of the Living* dead in contrast with sprinters of *28 Days Later* (Levin 2017); the speed at which the zombie moves may have a relevance to the rate at which an infection spreads as faster zombies could be more difficult to stop, resulting in more time to infect people. Fast zombies may also infect more people simply because they are better able to catch people.

Suppose we have data on the number of days it takes a zombie hunter to stop zombies from three separate zombie outbreaks under comparable conditions, with the only difference being the speed of the zombies as shown in Table 3.6.

Slow	Normal	Fast
7.9	10.6	11.9
8.7	11.1	8.2
9.6	9.8	17.6
10.3	14.6	14.6
9.3	15.3	13.7
10.6	10.4	16.2
8.8	14.9	10.6
9.3	9.3	15.8
7.1	13.1	13.5
11.5	12.7	15.3
7.6	8.8	11.6
8.9	13.6	11.5
9.8	9.3	15.6
9.7	11.2	13.7
8.1	12.3	8.6
9.0	10.7	13.0
	14.0	12.2
	13.2	15.7
	9.3	13.7
	15.8	
	14.7	
	13.0	

Table 3.6: Day from creation till being stopped

We could perform a 2-sample t-test if we were only comparing two means; however, we have three means to compare so we need to do an ANOVA. An ANOVA is much like a 2-sample t-test for more than 2 samples (Witte 1993). The name ANOVA stands for analysis of variance (McClave and Sincich 2009); however, it is a test of sample means and not sample variances.

To analyze the data, we got to **ANOVA > One-Way** and change the dropdown to "Response data are in a separate column for each factor level" and select the columns containing the data. Then click on **Graphs** and Select "Three in one." The resulting graph is shown in Figure 3.19. We check the probability plot to ensure the residuals are normally distributed and we observe the graphs to identify an unusual data points as they could strongly influence the results. In this case, the residuals plots look good.

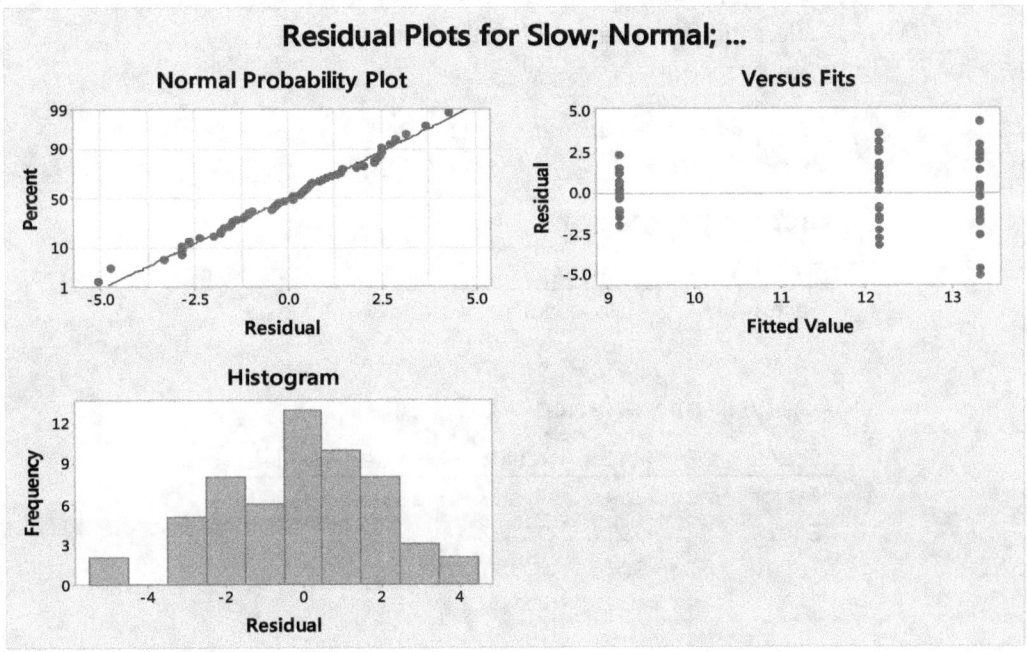

Figure 3.19: Residuals plot

Figure 3.20 shows the Minitab session widow for an ANOIVA. The P-value is less than 0.05 so we can conclude one or more means differs from the others. We know that there is a statistically significant difference between means, but we don't know where so we look at the interval lot in Figure 3.21.

One-way ANOVA: Slow; Normal; Fast

Method

Null hypothesis   All means are equal
Alternative hypothesis   Not all means are equal
Significance level   α = 0.05

Equal variances were assumed for the analysis.

Factor Information

Factor	Levels	Values
Factor	3	Slow; Normal; Fast

Analysis of Variance

Source	DF	Adj SS	Adj MS	F-Value	P-Value
Factor	2	159.9	79.953	18.10	0.000
Error	54	238.6	4.418		
Total	56	398.5			

Model Summary

S	R-sq	R-sq(adj)	R-sq(pred)
2.10193	40.13%	37.91%	33.61%

Means

Factor	N	Mean	StDev	95% CI
Slow	16	9.133	1.140	(8.080; 10.187)
Normal	22	12.160	2.213	(11.261; 13.058)
Fast	19	13.320	2.541	(12.353; 14.287)

Pooled StDev = 2.10193

Figure 3.20: Session window for ANOVA

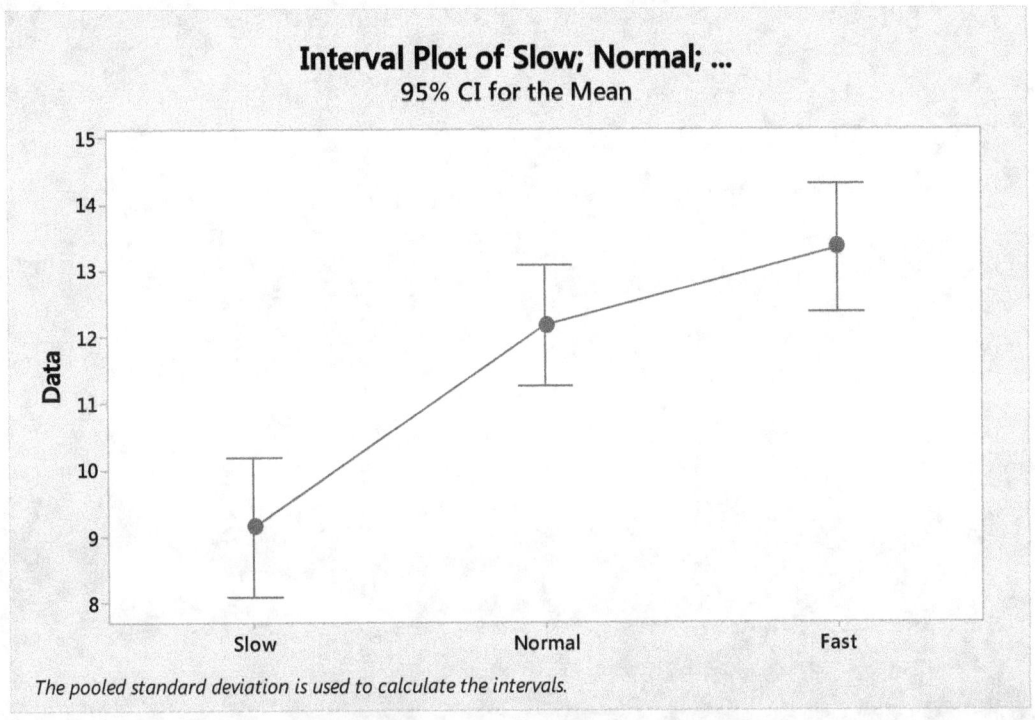

Figure 3.21: Interval plot

We see can see that the confidence interval for slow zombies does not overlap with the mean for normal or fast zombies. It seems that any academic study of zombies should take into consideration the speed at which the zombies move; otherwise, their conclusions may be incorrect.

This has been a hypothetical study. In the event of an actual zombie outbreak, we will either get actual data to do a real study, or all be turned into zombies, in which case we will no longer care about doing statistical studies. Think of it as a win-win situation.

CHAPTER 4

Regression Analysis

The proper way to perform a regression analysis is explained here using actual data from two case studies. The first example described a planned move in which data is used to determine if there is a potential relationship between estimated moving costs and the estimated number of boxes to move. The next example used a table of turkey weights and cooking times to determine the correct cooking time for a bird that was too small to be in the model. The hazards of extrapolating beyond the data set are also explained. The creation of a scatter plot is demonstrated.

The first example is of a regression analysis performed the usual way in Minitab; the second example shows how to use the Minitab assistant to perform the regression. The Minitab assistant guidance in interpreting results of a regression analysis for those who are not confident in their ability to perform a regression analysis. Using the Minitab assistant is a safer way to do things as the assistant helps with interpreting the results; however, the reader should not become dependent upon the assistant.

4.1 Regression Analysis: Moving On with Minitab

I recently moved, and right after finishing the less-than-joyous task of unpacking I decided to take and break and relax by playing with Minitab Statistical Software.

As a data source I used the many quotes I received from moving companies. I'd invited many companies to look around my previous home, and then they would provide me an estimate with the price in Euros as well as an estimate on the amount of goods that would need to be transported. The "amount of goods" estimate was given in boxes. I don't know what *size* boxes were referred to, but all the moving companies used boxes as a standard estimate of cubic area.

I had planned on using 35 boxes; most companies told me it would be 110-120 boxes. Since I was not even finished packing books when I had used up the first 50 boxes, I think I can safely assume the movers proved to be generally better at estimating shipping volume than I am.

Using Regression to Predict the Cost of Moving Let's suppose I wanted to determine the regression line for the cost of moving and the number of boxes that need to be moved. I rounded the estimates to the nearest 25 and changed the moving company names. Table 4.1 contains the estimates I received for cost and amount of goods.

Moving Company	Cost Estimate (in Euro)	Material Estimate (in Boxes)
Company A	1700	115
Company B	1850	120
Company C	3400	145
Company D	1650	80
Company E	1675	90
Company F	2000	110
Company G	1950	115

Table 4.1: Cost and material estimates

I was a bit suspicious of the estimate from Company C. The young man who gave me that estimate may not have even been born at a time when many of the other estimators where already working in the moving industry, so I wondered about his experience. Had the estimate been different, it may not have stood out, but his estimates were far higher than the others. Part of the reason this estimate was so high may be because he included extra costs for using a conveyor outside my window as a labor-saving device.

I would be happy to pay for a labor-saving device that *lowers* my overall costs, but I was not so happy with extra costs for an expensive labor saving device that actually raised the overall expense.

A Quick Visual Check of the Data I suspected Company C was an outlier, so to get a quick look at the situation I entered my data into a Minitab worksheet created a scatterplot by going to **Graph > Scatterplot** and selecting "Simple." I entered the column containing the cost estimate as the Y variable and the column containing the material estimate as the X variable. The resulting scatter plot is shown in Figure 4.1. The dot in the upper right hand corner is the result for Company C.

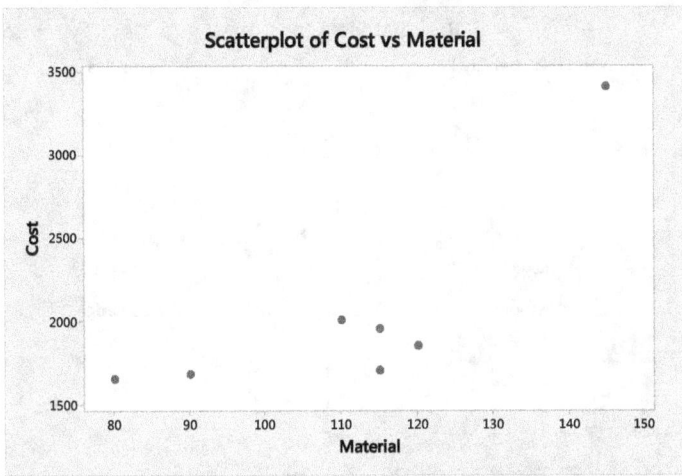

Figure 4.1: Scatter plot of cost versus material estimates

I am generally hesitant to discard potential outliers because I may be inadvertently throwing away valuable data, but in this case I decided that the estimates from Company C were just wrong and could throw off my regression model. Therefore, I was tempted to remove them from the data set, but decided to wait and see the results of the regression analysis.

Creating the Regression Model Regression analysis "involves predicting the value of one variable from one or more other variables. The dependent variable is sometimes called the response variable and the independent variable is called the predictor variable" (Weimer 1993 p. 622). In this example, the response variable is cost and the predictor variable is material.

Go to **Stat > Regression > Regression > Fit Regression Model** and entered Cost as the "Response" and Material as the "Continuous predictor." Then click on "Options" and select "Four in One" to view a graph with a:

- Histogram if residuals
- Normal probability plot of residuals
- Residuals versus firs
- Residuals versus order

The graph of residual plots shown in Figure 4.2 include a value that stands out as odd and the Minitab session window in Figure 4.3 shows a large residual for observation number 3, which is Comapyn C. I then removed company C and reran the regression.

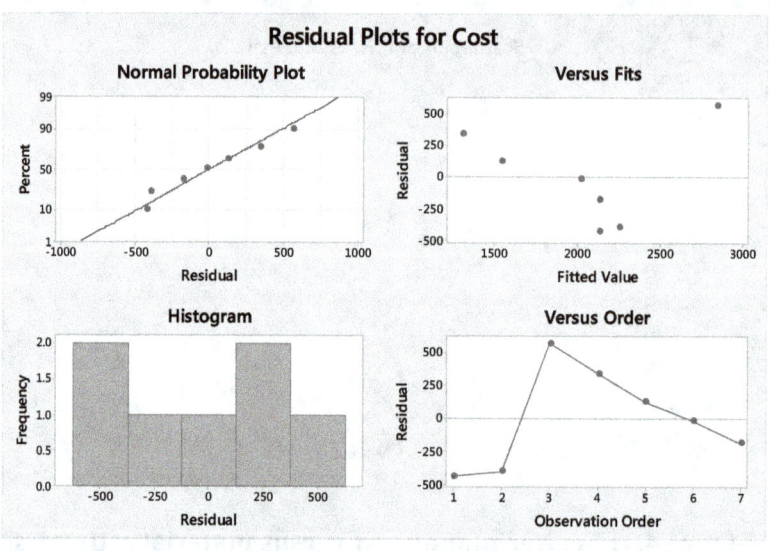

Figure 4.2: Graph of residual plots for cost

Regression Analysis: Cost versus Material

Analysis of Variance

Source	DF	Adj SS	Adj MS	F-Value	P-Value
Regression	1	1466413	1466413	8.84	0.031
Material	1	1466413	1466413	8.84	0.031
Error	5	829479	165896		
Lack-of-Fit	4	798229	199557	6.39	0.287
Pure Error	1	31250	31250		
Total	6	2295893			

Model Summary

S	R-sq	R-sq(adj)	R-sq(pred)
407.303	63.87%	56.65%	0.00%

Coefficients

Term	Coef	SE Coef	T-Value	P-Value	VIF
Constant	-562	886	-0.63	0.554	
Material	23.43	7.88	2.97	0.031	1.00

Regression Equation

Cost = -562 + 23.43 Material

Fits and Diagnostics for Unusual Observations

Obs	Cost	Fit	Resid	Std Resid	
3	3400	2835	565	2.15	R

R Large residual

Figure 4.3: Session window for regression analysis

The session window for the next regression analysis are shown in Figure 4.4. The residual plots in Figure X looked better and there were no unusual observations (see Fig. 4.5.); however, the P-value 0.163 and this indicates that the relationship between cost and material is not statistically significant.

Regression Analysis: Cost versus Material

Analysis of Variance

Source	DF	Adj SS	Adj MS	F-Value	P-Value
Regression	1	47704	47704	2.92	0.163
Material	1	47704	47704	2.92	0.163
Error	4	65317	16329		
Lack-of-Fit	3	34067	11356	0.36	0.804
Pure Error	1	31250	31250		
Total	5	113021			

Model Summary

S	R-sq	R-sq(adj)	R-sq(pred)
127.785	42.21%	27.76%	3.06%

Coefficients

Term	Coef	SE Coef	T-Value	P-Value	VIF
Constant	1168	376	3.11	0.036	
Material	6.06	3.54	1.71	0.163	1.00

Regression Equation

Cost = 1168 + 6.06 Material

Figure 4.4: Session window for regression analysis without Company C

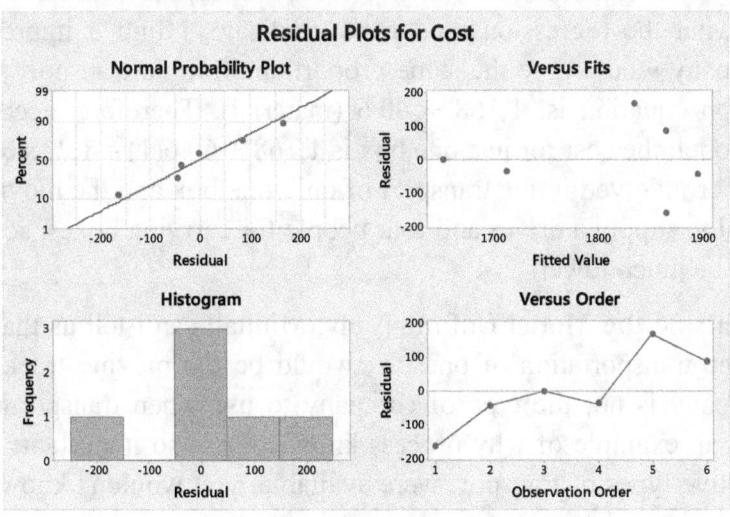

Figure 4.5: Graph of residual plots for cost without Company

The sample size of 6 was very small; therefore, even if the results were statistically significant, it would be difficult to precisely estimate the strength of the relationship. With a sample size under 15, it is important to check the plot of residuals to ensure the residuals are normally distributed. In this case, they appear to be, but the results were not statistically significant. However, this could change with more data, but I'm not willing to move again just to collect more data.

Cautions about Prediction with Regression Models There are some things to keep in mind when performing regression. This is a statistical calculation based on the *available* data. If my data set (the moving companies) is not be as inclusive as I think it is, the next moving company I contact may not match my sample. For example, two movers with an almost-falling-apart truck would generally charge much less than a luxury moving company that offers far more than just a transportation service.

We also need to be aware of the hazards of extrapolating beyond the data set (Keller, Warrack, and Bartel 1994). Suppose I bought an entire library full of books on statistics. I now have 400 boxes to transport and may be able to get a discount from a moving company that is happy to have such a large, but easy contract. The move may take a few trucks, but pre-packed books are faster to move than boxes full of fine china or large furniture items that need to be disassembled, and the price estimate would reflect this.

I am rather certain that this regression model will fall apart on the low side. The cost should go down as the number of boxes to transport is decreased; however, contrary to what the regression model may indicate, I find it improbable that a moving company would give the same proportional rate to transport just one box. The regression equation is: $1{,}168 + 60.6$ (material). Therefore, according to the regression model, the cost for just one box is $1{,}168 + 60.6(1) = 1{,}228.6$ Euro. There is far less labor involved in the transport of only one box and the moving company does not need to supply a driver and four people for carrying boxes, so the estimate may actually be much lower.

Thinking Outside the Model Unfortunately, Minitab can't tell us that the biggest expense in the transportation of one box would be the moving trucks' fuel, so a moving company is not the type of company to use when transporting only one box! This is an example of why process knowledge is so important: if you didn't know alternative types of transport were available, you wouldn't know the moving company was a poor choice for shipping one box!

Who knows, maybe someday Minitab will be able to do the all of the thinking for us! For now, whether calculating a regression model for costs/boxes or sales price/units, some knowledge of statistics and its limitations is still needed. Regression is an excellent way to make predictions and Minitab makes this easier; but it does not remove the need to have an understanding of the statistics being used.

4.2 A Six Sigma Master Black Belt in the Kitchen

I know that Thanksgiving is always on the last Thursday in November, but somehow, I failed to notice it was fast approaching until the Monday before Thanksgiving. This led to frantically sending a last-minute invitation, and a hunt for a turkey.

I live in Germany and this greatly complicated the matter. Not only is Thanksgiving not celebrated, but also actual turkeys are rather difficult to find.

I looked at a large grocery store's website and found 15 types of cat and dog food that *contain* turkey, but the only human food I could find was one jar of baby food.

Close, but not close enough. I wanted a whole turkey, not turkey puree.

The situation was even more complicated due to language: Germans have one word for a male turkey and a different word for a female turkey. I did not realize there was a difference, so I wound up only looking for a male turkey. My conversation with the store clerk would sound like this if it were translated into English, where there is only *one* word commonly used for turkey:

Me: Do you carry turkey?

Clerk: No. We only have turkey.

Me: I don't need turkey. I'm looking for turkey.

Clerk: Sorry, we don't carry turkey, but we have turkey if you want it.

Me: No thank you. I need turkey, not turkey.

Eventually, I figured out what happened and returned to buy the biggest female turkey they had. It weighed 5 pounds.

This was not the first time I cooked a turkey, but my first attempt resulted in The Great Turkey Fireball of 1998. (Cooking tip: Don't spray turkey juice onto the oven burner). My second attempt resulted in a turkey that still had ice in it after five hours in the oven. (Life hack: The inside of a turkey is a good place to keep ice from melting.)

This year, to be safe, I contacted an old friend who explained how to properly cook a turkey, but I was told I would need to figure out the cooking time on my own. This was not a problem...or so I thought. I looked online and found turkey cooking times for a stuffed turkey (Filippone 2017), but my turkey was too light to be included in the table.

Graphing the Data, I may not know much about cooking, but I do know statistics, so I decided to run a regression analysis to determine the correct cooking time for my bird. The weights and times were in a table (see Table 4.2) for ranges so I selected the times that corresponded to the low and high weight ranges and entered the data into a Minitab.

Weight	Time
6	3
8	3.5
12	4.5
16	5.5
20	6
24	6.5

Table 4.2: Weight and times

I like to look at my data before I analyze it so I created a scatterplot to see how time compares to weight. Go to **Graph > Scatter Plot** and select Simple. Enter Time as the "Y variable" and Weight as the "X variable." Visually (see Fig. 4.6), it looks as if there may be a relationship between weight and cooking time, so I then performed a regression analysis.

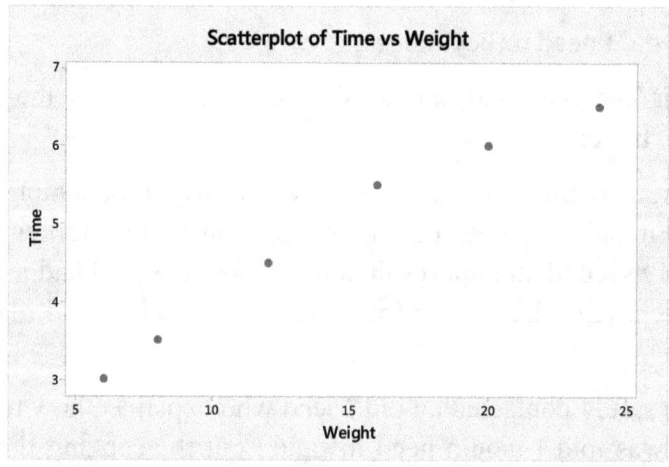

Figure 4.6: Scatter plot of weight and times

Performing Regression Analysis Go to **Stat > Regression > Regression > Fit Regression Model.** and select Time for the "Response" and Weight as the "Continuous predictor." Click on "Graphs" and select "Four in One."

The P-value is < 0.05 and the adjusted r-squared (adjusted) is 97.04% so it looks like I have a good model for time versus weight (See Fig. 4.7).

Regression Analysis: Time versus Weight

Analysis of Variance

Source	DF	Adj SS	Adj MS	F-Value	P-Value
Regression	1	9.6005	9.60046	164.90	0.000
Weight	1	9.6005	9.60046	164.90	0.000
Error	4	0.2329	0.05822		
Total	5	9.8333			

Model Summary

S	R-sq	R-sq(adj)	R-sq(pred)
0.241287	97.63%	97.04%	93.57%

Coefficients

Term	Coef	SE Coef	T-Value	P-Value	VIF
Constant	1.986	0.243	8.19	0.001	
Weight	0.1986	0.0155	12.84	0.000	1.00

Regression Equation

Time = 1.986 + 0.1986 Weight

Figure 4.7: Session window for regression analysis for time versus weight

The residual plots for time shown in Figure 4.8 include a normal probability plot with residuals that look like they are normally distributed. My data did not need to follow the normal distribution, but the residuals should. But something seemed odd to me when I looked at the other three plots. Suddenly, I was not so sure my model was as good as I thought it was.

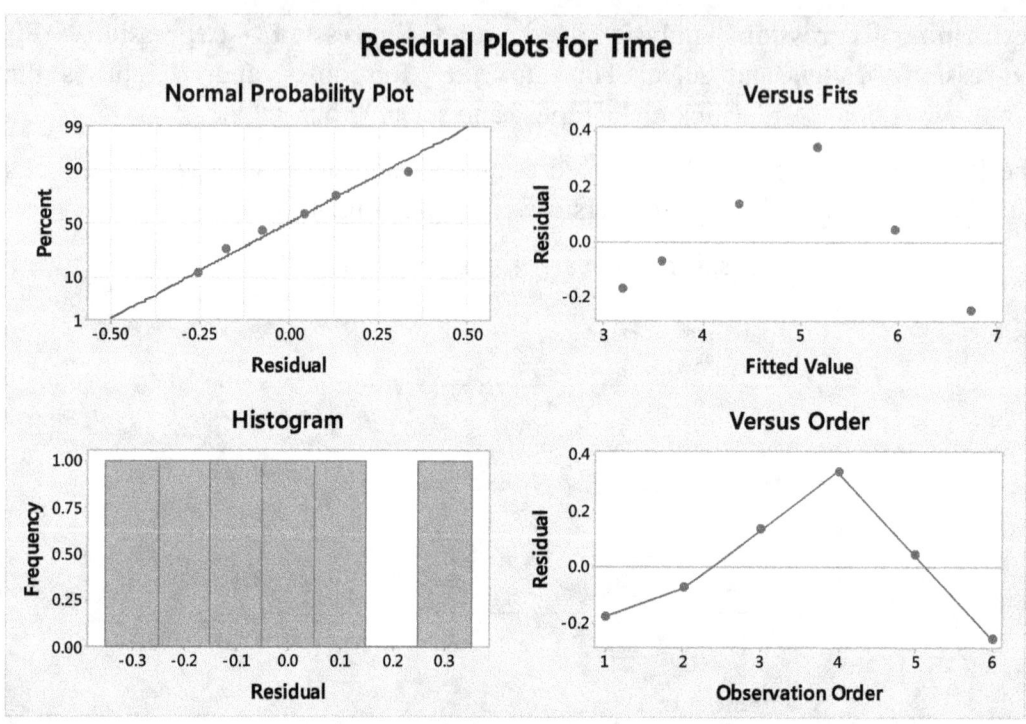

Figure 4.8: Residual plots for time

Regression Analysis with the Assistant I then used the Minitab Assistant to perform another regression analysis. Since I was uncertain about my first model, I could use the reports generated by the Assistant to better assess my data and the resulting analysis.

Go to **Assistant > Regression** and select "Simple Regression." Select Time for the "Y column" and Weight for the "X column" and select OK.

The first report provided by the Minitab Assistant is the summary report, shown in Figure 4.9. The report indicates a statistically significant relationship between time and weight using an Alpha of 0.05. It also tells me that 99.8% of the variability in time is caused by weight. This does not match my previous results and I can see why: I previously performed linear regression and the Minitab Assistant identified a quadratic model for the data.

The regression equation is Y = 0.9281 +0.3738X -0.005902(X^2).

Time = 0.9281 +0.3738(5) -0.005902(5^2) =

0.9281 + 1.869 − 1.869^2 =

2.7971 − 0.0008708401 = 2.796 hours

That means the cooking time is 2 hours and 48 minutes.

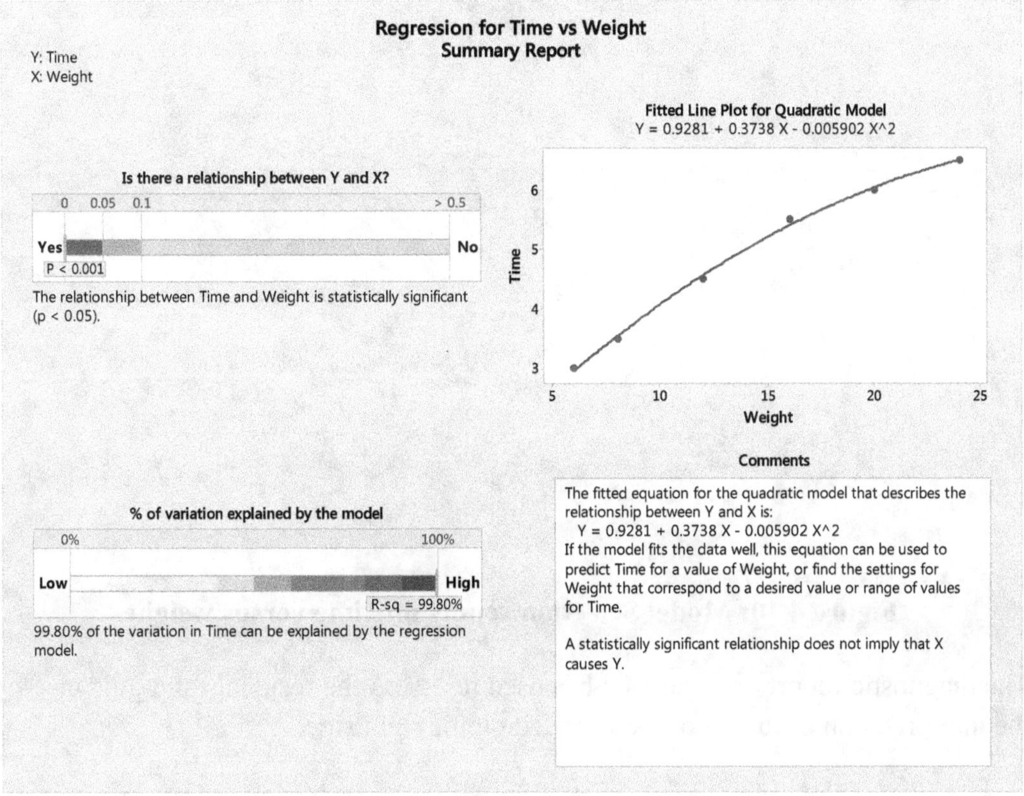

Figure 4.9: Summary report for time versus weight

Figure 4.10 depicts the model selection report, which includes a plot of the quadratic model and the r-squared (adjusted) for both the quadratic model and a linear model.

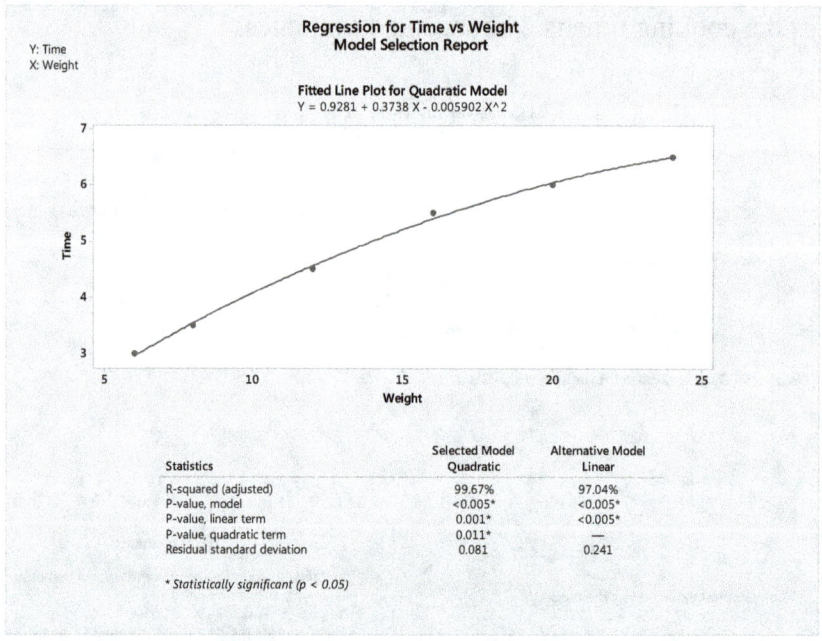

Figure 4.10: Model Selection report for time versus weight

The diagnostic report in Figure 4.11 is used to assess the residuals and guidance on the interpretation of the report is provided on the right side.

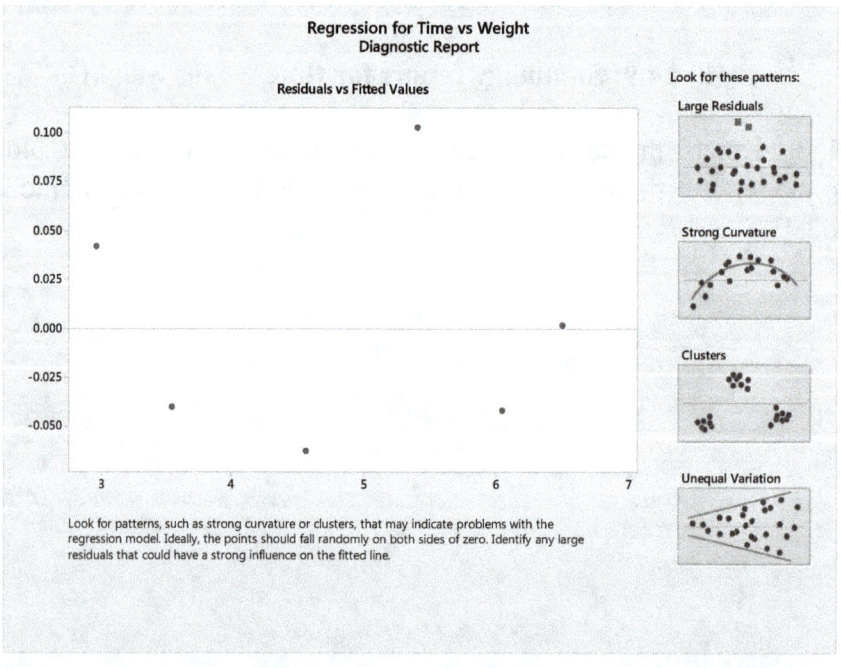

Figure 4.11: Diagnostic report for time versus weight

The prediction report in Figure 4.12 shows the prediction plot with the 95% prediction interval.

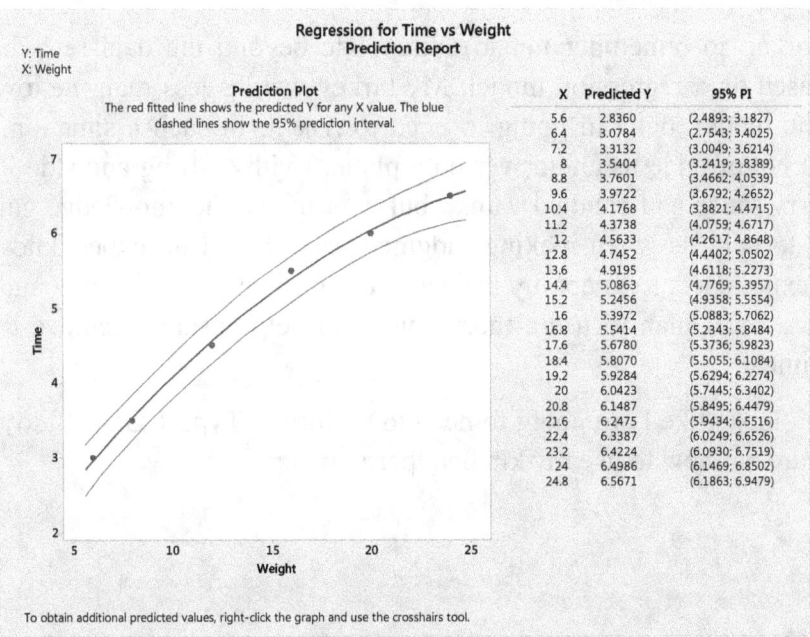

Figure 4.12: Prediction report for time versus weight

The report card shown in Figure 4.13 helps us to assess the suitability of the data. Here, I saw a problem: my sample size was only six. Minitab still provided me with results, but it warned me that the estimate for the strength of the relationship may not be very precise due to the low number if values I used. Minitab recommended I use 40 or more values. My data did not include any unusual data points, but using less than 15 values means the P-value could be incorrect if my results were not normally distributed.

Figure 4.13: Report card for time versus weight

It looks like my calculated cooking time may not be as accurate as I'd like it to be, but I don't think it will be too far off since the relationship between weights and cooking time is so strong.

It is important to remember not to extrapolate beyond the data set when taking actions based on a regression model. My turkey weighs less than the lowest value used in the model, but I'm going to need to risk it. In such a situation, statistics alone will not provide us an answer on a platter (with stuffing and side items such as cranberry sauce and candied yams), but we can use the knowledge gained from the study to help us when making judgment calls based on expert knowledge or previous experience. I expect my turkey to be finished in around two and a half to three hours, but I plan to use a thermometer to help ensure I achieve the correct cooking time.

But first, it looks like I am going to need to perform a Type 1 Gage Study analysis, once I figure out how to use my kitchen thermometer.

CHAPTER 5

Capability Studies

This chapter explains how to perform a capability study to determine if a process is statistically capable. Data created by using a model catapult was used to generate data to simulate manufacturing data. In place of measurements from parts, the distance of a projectile was measured and recorded. Multiple cycles of capability assessment are shown to simulate a process that is being optimized after each study. In addition to catapult study data, a hypothetical manufacturing example is presented. The concepts of process capability and process performance are also explained.

Minitab generates graphs when performing a capability and performance study. These graphs are shown and explained.

Simply entering values in Minitab and looking at the resulting capability value is not sufficient when performing a capability study. This chapter also explains how to assess the suitability of the data by ensuring the values are normally distributed, there is sufficient data available, and the process is in a state of statistical control.

5.1 Learning Process Capability Analysis with a Catapult

We can use a simple catapult to teach process capability analysis using Minitab Statistical Software's Capability Sixpack™. Here's how.

A process capability analysis is performed to determine if a process is statistically capable. Based on the results of the capability study, we can estimate the amount of defective components the process would produce.

However, a process must be in statistical control and have a normal distribution (Borror 2009). A process that is not in statistical control must be brought in control before the capability analysis is performed. In addition, data that does not fit the normal distribution will need to be normalized using a transformation such as the Box-Cox transformation.

The Catapult Setup and First Run A process and a specification are needed to demonstrate process capability analysis; we used a simple catapult. A rough idea of the catapult's range and precision was required for determining what the specification should be, so we fired five catapult shots and recorded the distance the projectile traveled. Based on the results, we determined the catapult should be able to consistently land projectiles within a range of one meter. This was just a rough figure used to get started.

We set the specification at 700 cm from the end of a hallway to the point where the projectiles should land. The tolerance was set as +/- 50 cm, which might or might not be a specification that the catapult could meet. The purpose of the study was to determine if the catapult is capable, so the uncertainty was not a problem.

The catapult was then set up 400 cm away from the target of 700 cm.

The First Run and Capability Analysis The catapult has a rubber band that hooks onto the front of the catapult and then goes over a wire guide that causes additional stretching before the rubber band is mounted onto the catapult arm. The wire guide was replaced with a thin wire that was bent and distorted. Ten shots were fired and the results were recorded. The wire was rotated 22.5° after each shot; rotating a weak and bent wire simulated a cause of variation in the process. The data was entered into a data collection sheet set up for the data to be entered into Minitab in subgroups of 5 as shown in Table 5.1.

SG1	642	721	663	687	673
SG2	741	658	672	749	726
SG3	656	737	662	650	682
SG4	701	753	663	686	729
SG5	676	668	674	643	651
SG6	725	650	694	723	698
SG7	654	660	658	703	651
SG8	723	660	705	649	652
SG9	725	646	658	696	735
SG10	646	674	679	643	683
SG11	757	714	661	657	746
SG12	670	648	751	637	748
SG13	715	690	724	724	682
SG14	673	783	637	637	728
SG15	748	640	771	668	700

SG16	641	709	731	751	684
SG17	657	654	710	658	678
SG18	649	706	671	674	680
SG19	691	691	637	706	748
SG20	697	661	709	702	677

Table 5.1: Weak wire data

Go to **Quality Tools > Capability Sixpack > Normal** and select "Subgroups across rows of" and then select the columns containing the data. Then, enter the lower specification of 650 and the upper specification of 750.

The Minitab Capability Sixpack results for the run using a thin wire are depicted in Figure 5.1. Minitab's Capability Sixpack provides an Xbar chart, an R chart, a view of the last five subgroups, a capability histogram, a normal probability plot and a capability plot with capability indices.

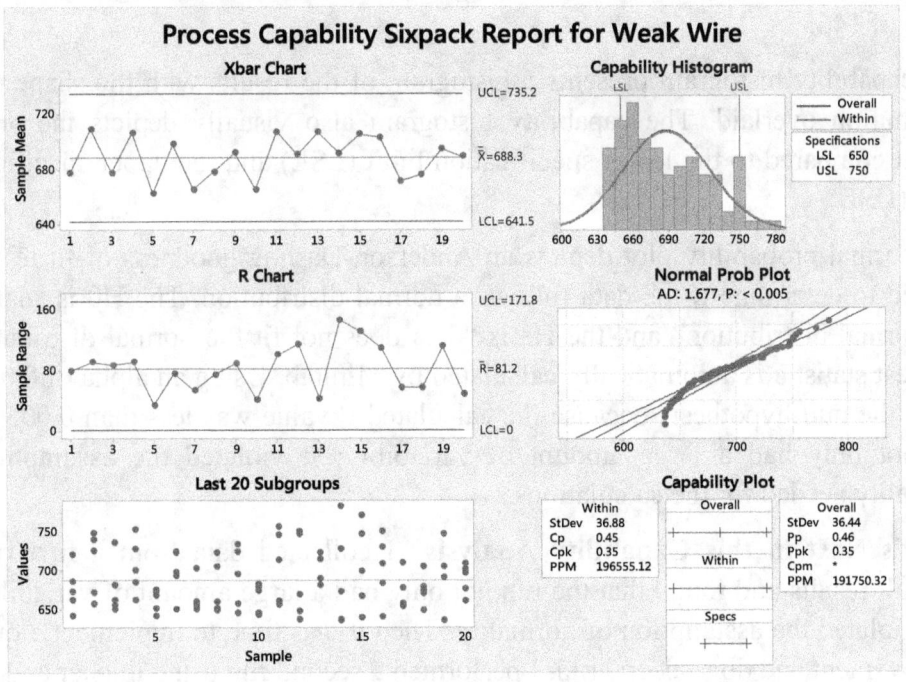

Figure 5.1: Process capability Sixpack for weak wire

The Xbar chart and R chart were automatically calculated by Minitab using the run data that was entered. The specified subgroup size was five, so each dot in the Xbar chart represents the average of five catapult shots. The average of the averages is 688.3 cm. This is short of the target of 700 cm, but still within specification.

Unfortunately, while the mean was within the specification limits, many values were not.

Minitab has calculated the upper control limit (UCL) and lower control limit (LCL). The control limits are 3σ above or below the mean. The UCL is 735.2 cm and the lower control limit is 641.5 cm. The average was within the specification; however, the control limits are +/- 3σ of the process mean and 99.7% of the sample means will be within the control limits. Unfortunately, the catapult process will result in shots that will be out of specification because the LCL is below the LSL.

Reading the Process Capability Charts The R chart calculates the average of the ranges in each subgroup of sample size five. The UCL and LCL for the range can be calculated using the average of the ranges and a table; however, Minitab automatically performs the calculations. Here, we can observe a large amount of variation in the catapult results. The actual results of the last 20 subgroups are also given. The difference between the first and second shot fired was almost 80 cm; hence, the large range for the first subgroup in the R chart. Subgroup 14 had a range of 146!

The capability histogram presents a histogram of the results with the shape of the distribution overlaid. The capability histogram also visually depicts the process output compared to the lower specification limit (LSL) and the upper specification limit (USL).

The normal probability plot depicts an Anderson-Darling goodness-of-fit test; this is used to determine if the data follows a normal distribution. The H0 is "data fits the normal distribution" and the Ha is "data does not fit the normal distribution." The test statistic is automatically calculated by Minitab. Using an alpha of 0.05, we reject the null hypothesis because the calculated P value was less than 0.005. This run not only had a large amount of variability; it violated the assumption of normality needed for the calculations.

What's Next in this Capability Analysis? I collected data from a first run of catapult results and found that the run not only had a large amount of variability, it also violated the assumption of normality. Then it was time to implement a quality improvement and do a second run. I performed a second run using thicker and more robust wire to stretch the rubber band. Since this wire will not have the variation that the thin one did, it was used to simulate a process improvement. We should see a reduction in variability as a result.

The Second Run and Capability Analysis A second run was performed using thicker and more robust wire to stretch the rubber band; this wire did not have the variation that the first one did, so it simulates a process improvement that should reduce variability. The new results are shown in Table 5.2.

SG1	644	680	687	693	676
SG2	688	655	666	680	697
SG3	684	701	667	642	669
SG4	723	668	680	678	721
SG5	678	687	651	670	687
SG6	663	673	692	664	650
SG7	669	671	656	688	685
SG8	679	716	680	670	691
SG9	655	687	678	681	683
SG10	681	666	661	713	664
SG11	701	655	679	671	669
SG12	685	687	689	672	688
SG13	677	675	692	679	694
SG14	649	699	658	696	680
SG15	665	681	659	666	684
SG16	705	654	643	662	667
SG17	641	673	662	686	712
SG18	691	689	665	678	685
SG19	659	681	655	680	698
SG20	667	643	680	667	688

Table 5.2: Strong wire data

The results are depicted in the Capability Sixpack shown in Figure 5.1. The Xbar chart for this run shows the UCL is below the USL; unfortunately, although the LCL is now above the LSL, there are still shots that landed below the lower specification limit. Also, the capability histogram indicates the normal distribution for this run is wider than the specification limits.

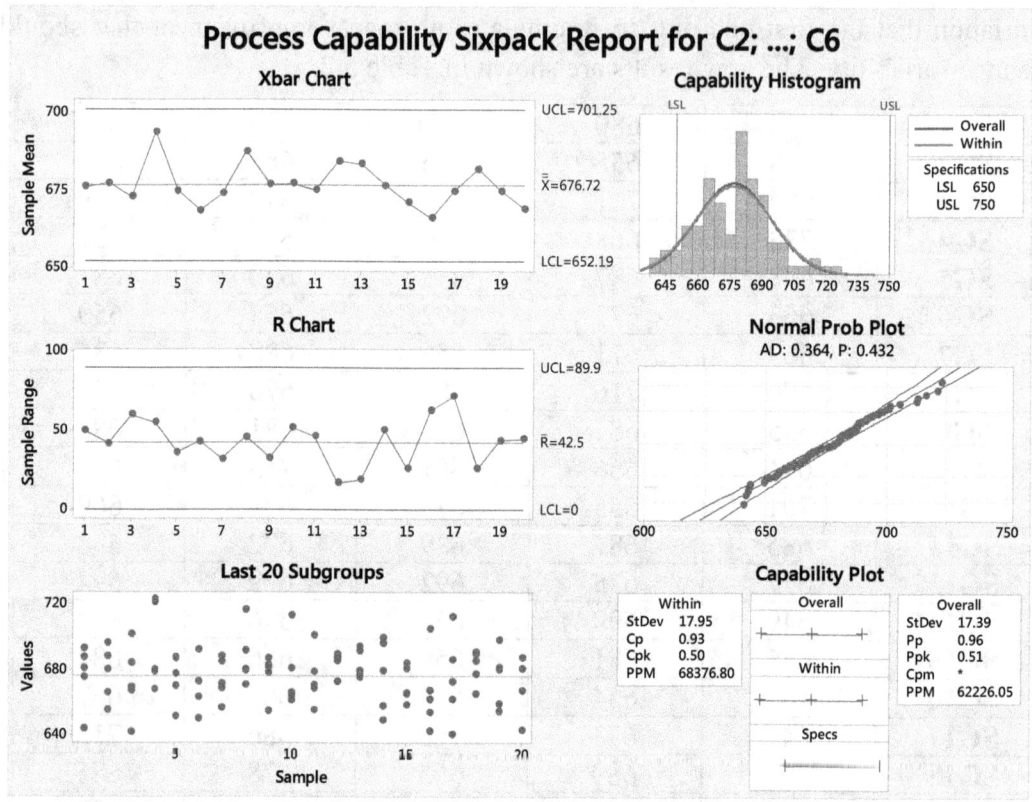

Figure 5.2: Process capability Sixpack for strong wire

The normal probability plot has a P value of 0.432 so we fail to reject the null hypothesis, which we stated as "data fits the normal distribution." The normal probability plot indicates the data fits the assumption of normality so we move on to the capability plot.

Differences Between Within and Overall Indices in a Capability Analysis
There are results for "within" and "overall" indices. The difference between within and overall is the way in which the process variation is estimated. Within variation only common cause variation in subgroups in the calculation and overall variation includes both common cause and special cause variation for the entire set of data from the process study. Common cause variation results from the system and special cause variation results from an assignable cause (Durivage 2015). The manipulation of the weak wire would be an example of a special cause.

The within indices are the capability indices C_p and C_{pk} and they can be thought of as what the process is capable of producing. The overall indices are P_p and P_{pk} and they are the processes' actual performance with the possible presence of variation due to special cause.

A C_p is a process capability index used to determine if a process is capable of meeting a specification. It is determined by dividing the tolerance range by six times the standard deviation.

$$C_p = \frac{USL-LSL}{6\sigma}$$

Ideally, a C_p should be 1.33 or greater as this would mean the spread of the data is only 75% of the tolerance range; this leaves room for slight variations in the process without generating out-of-specification parts. However, the C_p index does not tell us if the process would produce parts that are within specification. A process could have a C_p of 2.00 due to very little variation, but still be producing out of specification parts because the process mean is at the edge of a specification limit.

A more complete picture is provided by also using the C_{pk} index, which is based on two calculations. The first calculation is USL minus the process mean divided by three times the process standard deviation, and the second calculation is the process mean minus LSL divided by three times the process standard deviation.

$$C_{pk} = \frac{USL-\bar{X}}{3\sigma} \text{ and } \frac{\bar{X}-LSL}{3\sigma}$$

The lower of the two results is used to identify the process capability in regards to the centering of the process in comparison to the specification limits. Like C_p, a C_{pk} should generally be 1.33 or greater.

The formulas for P_p and P_{pk} are somewhat similar to the C_p and C_{pk} formulas; however, calculations for P_p and P_{pk} use the process variation in place of the standard deviation.

$$P_p = \frac{USL-LSL}{6s} \qquad P_{pk} = \frac{USL-\bar{X}}{3s} \text{ and } \frac{\bar{X}-LSL}{3s}$$

The Minitab Capability Sixpack results for the second run indicate a P_p of 0.0.96 and a P_{pk} of 0.51 and a Cp of 0.93 and a Cpk of 0.50. These results are much lower than the ideal of 1.33. Minitab has determined the process would result in a parts per million (PPM) of 68,376.80. This means that over 68,000 out-of-specification catapult shots can be expected for every 1,000,000 shots. This corresponds to a defect rate of 6.8%.

Even if none of the shots we made were out of specification, the process is still not capable and would need improvement.

The Third Run and Process Capability Analysis

The means of the previous run were spread around a mean of 677 cm so the catapult process was adjusted by moving the catapult 20 centimeters closer to the target area. Another 100 shots were fired the new data was analyzed (see Table 5.3).

SG1	716	712	706
SG2	715	678	696
SG3	685	698	716
SG4	703	716	685
SG5	684	682	713
SG6	700	716	675
SG7	714	692	695
SG8	691	701	724
SG9	720	685	703
SG10	713	687	677
SG11	714	691	727
SG12	711	712	674
SG13	682	711	673
SG14	718	688	690
SG15	715	680	700
SG16	661	709	677
SG17	691	714	708
SG18	707	692	707
SG19	663	695	681
SG20	702	707	701

Table 5.3: Process improvement data

The results show an improvement as depicted in Figure 5.3. The Xbar control limits are now within the range of the specification limits and both P_p and P_{pk} have improved. The PPMs indicate a defect rate of only 0.3%; this is an improvement, but still not acceptable for ensuring a product that conforms to specification in a mass-production environment. A manufacturing company with a C_p of 1.00 and a production run of 10,000 units should anticipate around 30 units out of specification. The catapult process needs further improvements to reduce variation; fortunately, there are quality tools available to help with this.

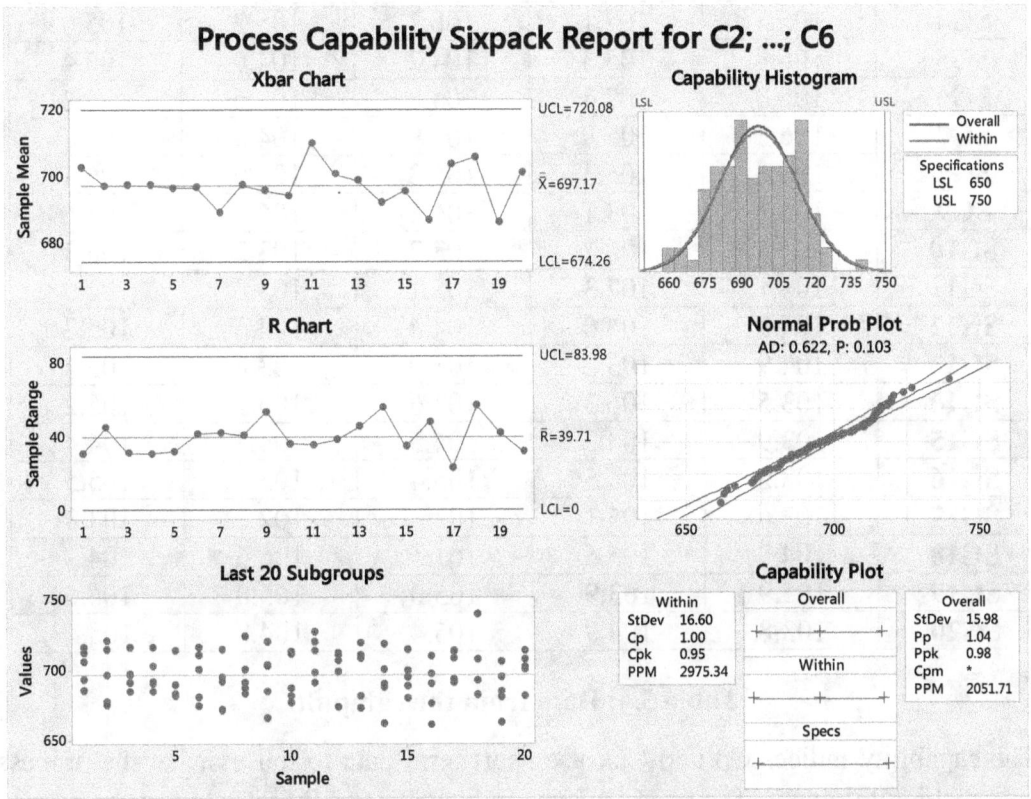

Figure 5.3: Process capability Sixpack for process improvement

5.2 Using a Catapult as a Minitab Capability Sixpack Training Aid

Teaching process performance and capability studies is easier when actual process data is available for the student or trainee to practice with and a catapult can be used to generate data for a capability study. The catapult is can be used in various configurations, but here the settings will stay constant to simulate a manufacturing process.

The Catapult Study The catapult used a 120 mm diameter heavy-duty rubber band originally intended for use in model airplanes. The rubber band guide was set at 4 cm and the arm stopper was set at 1 cm. The starting point was set at 8 cm and these settings were held constant for the duration of the study. Three operators each performed 2 runs of 20 shots each to simulate two days of production with three shifts per day. Each run was used a separate subgroup in the capability and performance study. The catapult data is shown in Table 5.4.

SG1	105.3	104.3	104.3	107.5	105.9
SG2	105.2	104.9	106.2	105.9	104.4
SG3	105.8	105.8	104.3	102.2	105.4
SG4	105.5	107.1	106.1	105.2	105.6
SG5	106.7	105.3	104.2	104.9	105.4
SG6	105.0	107.4	104.8	103.6	105.2
SG7	106.2	105.9	105.9	104.2	104.7
SG8	104.6	105.3	105.3	105.9	106.3
SG9	105.1	103.1	104.5	106.4	103.6
SG10	105.3	105.7	103.7	103.2	105.3
SG11	104.1	107.3	105.1	103.4	104.9
SG12	104.9	104.0	104.4	104.6	105.2
SG13	104.9	103.2	105.9	103.6	103.4
SG14	103.5	106.3	104.6	106.1	105.2
SG15	103.9	103.2	104.5	104.4	104.4
SG16	103.5	104.5	105.4	105.1	105.5
SG17	103.6	105.1	103.8	102.2	103.3
SG18	104.8	105.5	103.5	106.6	104.7
SG19	105.9	103.9	105.0	105.0	106.6
SG20	103.8	104.9	105.4	104.8	105.4

Table 5.4: Data from the catapult

The capability indices Cp and Cpk use short-term data to tell us what the process sis capable of doing and the performance indices Pp and Ppk use long-term data to tell us what the process is actually doing. The capability indices use "within" variation in the formula and performance indexes use "overall" variation; within variation is based on the pooled standard deviations of the subgroups and overall variation is based on the standard deviation of the entire data set.

There are requirements that must be met to perform a capability or performance study. The data must be normally distributed and the process needs to be in a state of statistical control. The data must also be randomly selected and it needs to represent the population (Gryna 2001). There should be at least 100 values in the data set; otherwise, there will be a very wide confidence interval for the resulting capability and performance values (Breyfogle 2003). The person planning the study must ensure there is sufficient data and the data represents the values in the population; however, the Capability Sixpack can be used to ensure the other requirements are fulfilled.

Go to **Quality Tools > Capability Sixpack > Normal** and select "Subgroups across rows of" and then select the columns containing the data. Then, enter the lower specification of 95 and the upper specification of 110. Click on Options and add a Target of 104. The resulting Capability Sixpack graph is shown in Figure 5.4.

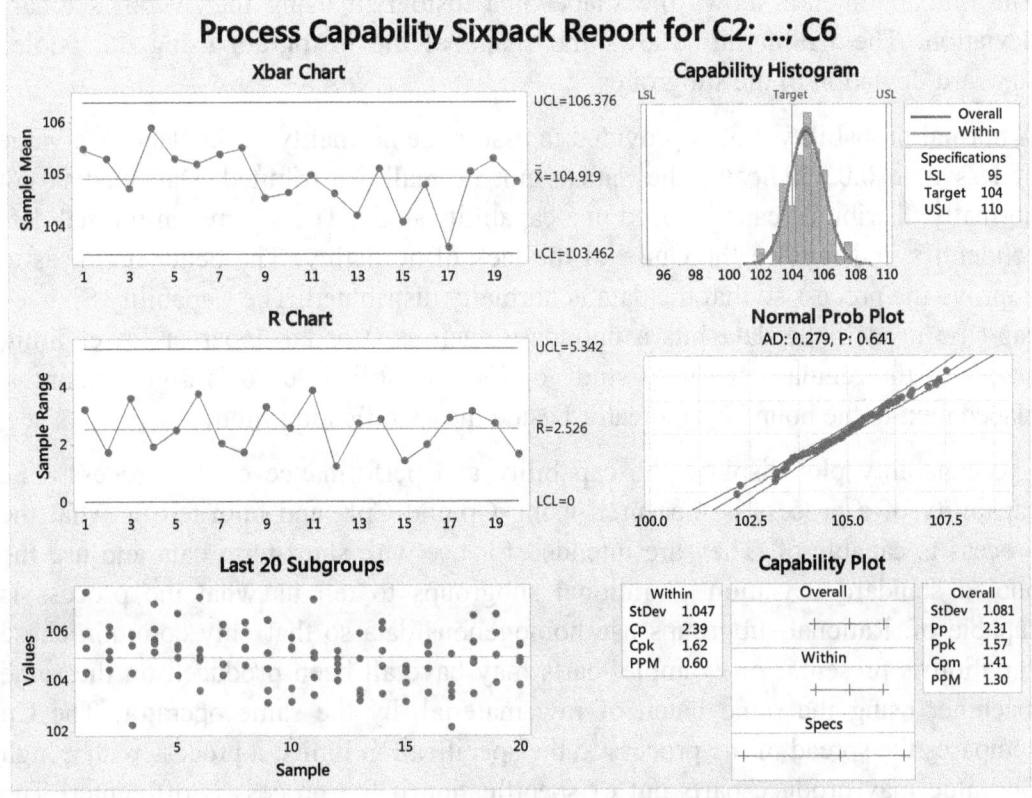

Figure 5.4: Catapult study Capability Sixpack

The Capability Sixpack The Capability Sixpack provides an I chart when the data consists of individual values; i.e. the subgroup size is 1. An Xbar chart is provided when the data is entered as subgroups. Either control chart can be used to assess the stability of the process. The process will need improvement to achieve stability if out of control values are seen in a control chart. The source of the variability in the process should be sought out and removed and then the study should be repeated.

A moving range chart is given when the subgroup sizes is 1 and an R chart is given when the subgroup size is greater than 1. The values in the moving range chart should be compared to the values in the I chart to ensure no patterns are present. The same should be done for the Xbar and R chart if they are used. This is done to help ensure the data are truly random. Either the last 25 observations or the last 20 subgroups will be shown. The last 25 observations are shown if the data is entered as 1 subgroup and the last 20 subgroups are shown if the data are entered as subgroups. The values should appear random and without trends or shifts if the process is stable.

A capability histogram is shown to compare the histogram of the data to the specification limits. The data should approximate the standard normal distribution. The line for overall shows the shape of a histogram using the overall standard deviation. The within line shows the shape of the histogram using the pooled standard deviation of the subgroups.

A normal probability plot is provided to assess the normality of the data. A p value of less than 0.05 indicates the data is not normally distributed. Data that is not normally distributed can't be used in a capability study. Transform non-normal data or identify and remove the cause of the lack of normality. The better option is to improve the process so that the data is normally distributed. The Capability Sixpack can't be used if the data hits a boundary such as 0 or an upper or lower limit; however, the regular capability study option can still be used is a checkmark is placed next to the boundary indicator beside the specification limit.

The capability plot displays the capability and performance of the process. The capability of a process is measured using Cp and CpK and both tell us what the process is capable of. They are intended for use with short-term data and use the pooled standard deviation of rational subgroups to tell us what the process is capable of. Rational subgroups use homogenous data so that only common cause variation is present. For example, parts may have all been produced on the same machine, using the same batch of raw material, by the same operator. The Cp compares the spread of the process to the specification limits; a process with a high Cp value may produce parts out of specification if the process is off-center. The Cpk considers position of the process mean relative to specification limits and there are actually two values for Cpk, the Cpk of the upper speciation limit and the Cp of the lower specification limit. The Capability Sixpack lists the value of the worse performing of the two Cp values.

The performance of a process is measured using Pp and Ppk with long-term data. Generally, more than 30-days' worth of production data should be used for Pp and Ppk. Unlike the capability indices Cp and Cpk, Pp and Ppk calculations are performed using the total standard deviation, which is the same as the formula for a sample standard deviation. The Pp compares the spread of the process to the upper and lower specification limits and only the worse performing value is given. The Ppk considers position of the process mean relative to specification limits.

The process capability index of the mean is the Cpm, which uses a target value to account for the process mean relative to the target. However, this is only given if a target value is entered in Minitab.

Conclusion The Minitab Capability Sixpack will quickly and easily provide a capability study; however, it will not tell you if the data is unstable for a capability study. It does however provide methods for assessing the suitability of the data and they should be used every time a capability study is performed.

5.3 Strangest Capability Study: Super-Zooper-Flooper-Do Broom Boom

The great Dr. Seuss tells of Mr. Plunger, who is the custodian at Diffendoofer School on the corner of Dinkzoober and Dinzott in the town of Dinkerville. The good Mr. Plunger "keeps the whole school clean" using a supper-zooper-flooper-do (Dr. Seuss, Prelutsky, and Smith 1998).

Unfortunately, Dr. Seuss fails to tell us where the supper-zooper-flooper-do came from and if the production process was capable.

Let's assume the broom boom length was the most critical dimension on the supper-zooper-flooper-do. The broom boom length drawing calls for a length of 55.0 mm with a tolerance of +/- 0.5 mm. The quality engineer has checked three supper-zooper-flooper-do broom booms and all were in specification, so he concludes that there is no reason to worry about the process producing out of specification parts. But we know this not true. Perhaps the fourth supper-zooper-flooper-do broom boom *will* be out of specification. Or maybe the 1,000[th].

It's time for a capability study, but don't fire up your Minitab Statistical Software just yet. First we need to plan the capability study. Each day the supper-zooper-flooper-do factory produces supper-zooper-flooper-do broom booms with a change in broom boom material batch every 50th part. A capability study should have a minimum of 100 values (Hare 2007) and 25 subgroups. The subgroups should be rational: that means the variability within each subgroup should be less than the variability between subgroups. We can anticipate more variation between material batches than within a material batch so we will use the batches as subgroups, with a sample size of four. The results are shown in Table 5.5.

Observation	Length	Observation	Length	Observation	Length	Observation	Length	Observation	Length
1	55.08	21	55.12	41	55.26	61	54.94	81	55.15
2	55.19	22	55.35	42	55.18	62	55.29	82	55.17
3	55.25	23	55.16	43	55.07	63	55.10	83	55.23
4	55.06	24	55.24	44	55.24	64	55.15	84	55.23
5	55.29	25	55.04	45	54.95	65	55.19	85	55.22
6	55.1	26	55.0	46	55.0	66	55.1	86	55.2

	.3		.9		.9		.3		.3
7	55.22	27	55.25	47	55.15	67	55.10	87	55.02
8	55.08	28	54.96	48	55.02	68	55.23	88	55.18
9	55.11	29	54.99	49	55.29	69	55.09	89	55.19
10	55.09	30	55.27	50	55.22	70	55.12	90	55.11
11	55.25	31	55.25	51	55.13	71	55.21	91	55.25
12	55.05	32	55.21	52	55.16	72	55.17	92	55.09
13	55.28	33	55.12	53	55.46	73	55.03	93	55.11
14	55.20	34	55.21	54	55.12	74	55.04	94	54.90
15	55.32	35	55.11	55	55.31	75	55.04	95	55.04
16	55.30	36	55.14	56	55.05	76	55.10	96	55.18
17	55.34	37	55.28	57	55.16	77	55.16	97	55.29
18	55.11	38	55.14	58	55.12	78	55.12	98	55.24
19	55.04	39	55.16	59	55.19	79	55.27	99	55.14
20	55.22	40	55.11	60	55.14	80	55.10	100	55.31

Table 5.5: Broom boom length measurements

Once the data has been collected, we can crank up our Minitab and perform a capability study by going to **Stat > Quality Tools > Capability Analysis > Normal**. Enter the column containing the measurement values. Then either enter the column containing the subgroup or type the size of the subgroup; in this case, the subgroup size was 4. Enter the lower specification limit and the upper specification limit, and click OK. The resulting graph is shown in Figure 5.5.

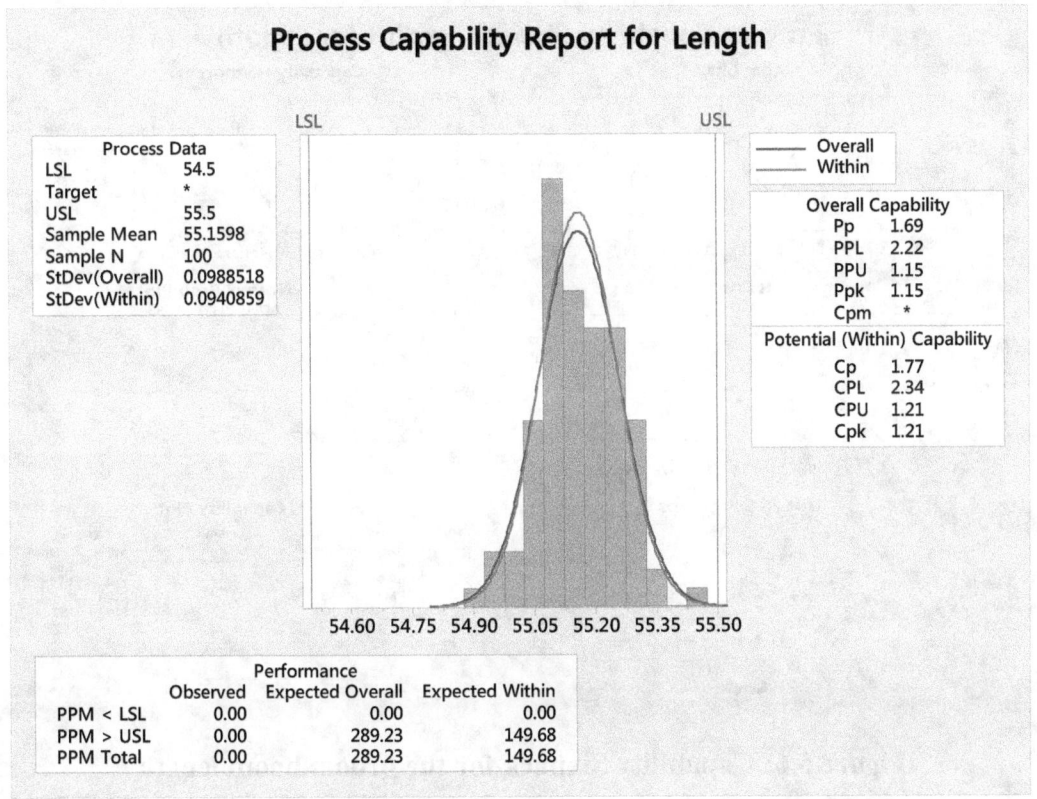

Figure 5.5: Capability analysis for the broom boom length

We now have the results for the supper-zooper-flooper-do broom boom lengths, but can we trust our results? A capability study has requirements that must be met. We should have a minimum of 100 values and 25 subgroups, which we have. But the data should also be normally distributed and in a state of statistical control; otherwise, we either need to transform the data, or identify the distribution of the data and perform capability study for nonnormal data.

Dr. Seuss has never discussed transforming data so perhaps we should be hesitant if the data do not fit a distribution. Before performing a transformation, we should determine if there is a reason the data do not fit any distribution.

We can use the Minitab Capability Sixpack to determine if the data is normally distributed and in a state of statistical control. Go to **Stat > Quality Tools > Capability Sixpack > Normal**. Enter the column containing the measurement values. Then either enter the column containing the subgroup or type the size of the subgroup. Enter the lower specification limit and the upper specification limit and click OK. The resulting graph is shown in Figure 5.6.

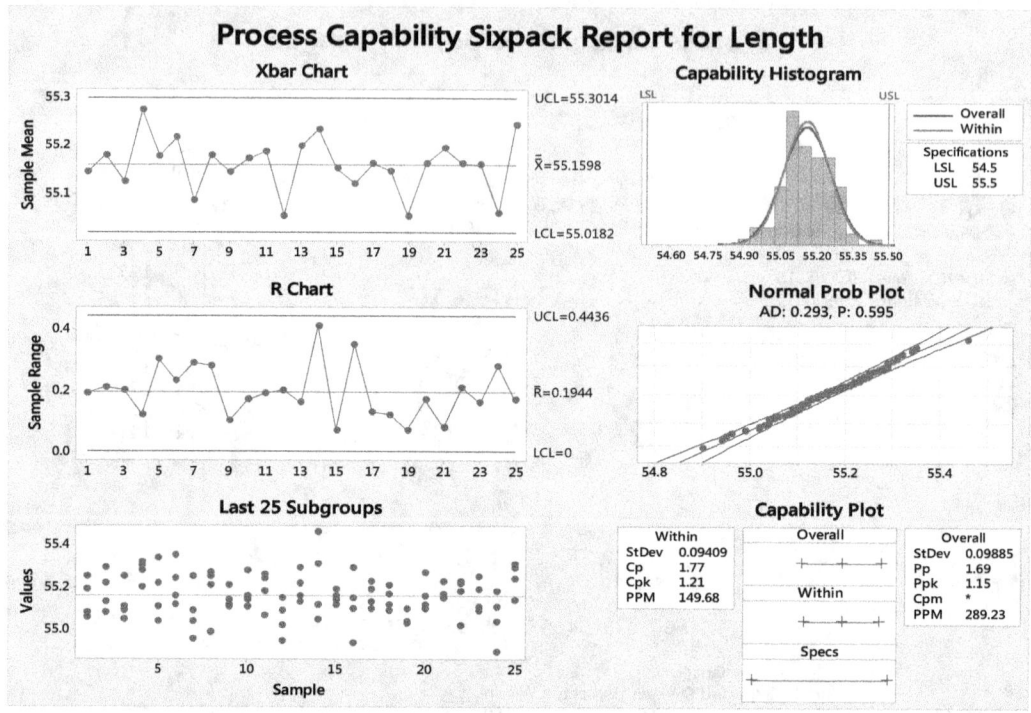

Figure 5.6: Capability Sixpack for the broom boom length

There are no out-of-control points in the control chart and the normal probability plot follows a straight line, and has a P value is greater than 0.05, so we fail to reject the null hypothesis that the data follow a normal distribution. The data is suitable for a capability study.

The within subgroup variation is also known as short term capability and is indicated by Cp and Cpk. The between subgroup variability is also known as long term capability is given as Pp and Ppk. The Cp and Cpk fail to account for the variability that will occur between batches; Pp and Ppk tell us what we can expect from the process over time.

Both Cp and Pp tell us how well the process conforms to the specification limits. In this case, a Cp of 1.63 tells us the spread of the data is much narrower than the width of the specification limits, and that is a good thing. But Cp and Pp alone are not sufficient. The Cpk and Ppk indicate how spread out the data is relative to the center of the specification limits. There is an upper and lower Cpk and Ppk; however, we are generally only concerned with the lower of the two values.

In the supper-zooper-flooper-do broom boom length example, a Cpk of 1.10 is an indication that the process is off center. The Cp is 1.63, so we can reduce the number of potentially out-of-specification supper-zooper-flooper-do broom booms if we shift the process mean down to center the process while maintaining the current variation. This is a fortunate situation as it is often easier to shift the process mean than to reduce the process variation.

Once improvements are implemented and verified, we can be sure that the next supper-zooper-flooper-do the Diffendoofer School purchases for Mr. Plunger will have a broom boom that is in specification if only common cause variation is present.

CHAPTER 6

Statistical Process Control

Statistical Process Control is introduced. The critical concepts of common cause variability and special cause variability are introduced along with an explanation of the consequences of confusing the two. Creating an individuals chart is shown; this is followed by an introduction of the Nelson rules for control charts. The Nelson rules are used to identify out of control points on a control chart; however, activating all of them at the same time increases the risk of falsely identifying values as out of statistical control. Guidance on activating the various Nelson rules in Minitab is provided.

The various types of control charts are presented and guidance is given for selecting the correct type of control chart for an intended use. The concepts of variable and attribute data are also described as this must be understood to correctly select a control chart for a given type of data.

6.1 Using the Nelson Rules for Control Charts in Minitab

Control charts plot your process data to identify and distinguish between common cause and special cause variation. This is important, because identifying the different causes of variation lets you take action to make improvements in your process without *over*-controlling it. Unneeded process changes, such as treating common cause variation as special cause variation, is knowing as tampering and it could lead to a process going out of control (Kubiak and Benbow 2009).

When you create a control chart, the software you're using should make it easy to see where you may have variation that requires your attention. For example,

Practical Statistical Methods for Quality

Minitab Statistical Software automatically flags any control chart data point that is more than three standard deviations above the centerline, as shown in the I chart in Figure X. To create the I chart using the data in Table X, go to **Control Charts > Variables Control Charts for Individuals > Individuals** and enter the column containing the data. The data in Table 6.1 was used to create the control chart shown in Figure 6.1.

Data
15.48
15.58
15.45
15.29
15.18
15.22
15.20
15.33
15.39
15.34
15.43
15.53
15.29
15.31
15.32
15.33
15.36
15.38
15.39
15.60
15.41
15.51
15.49
15.29
15.43
15.72
15.38
15.35
15.41
15.36

Table 6.1: I chart data

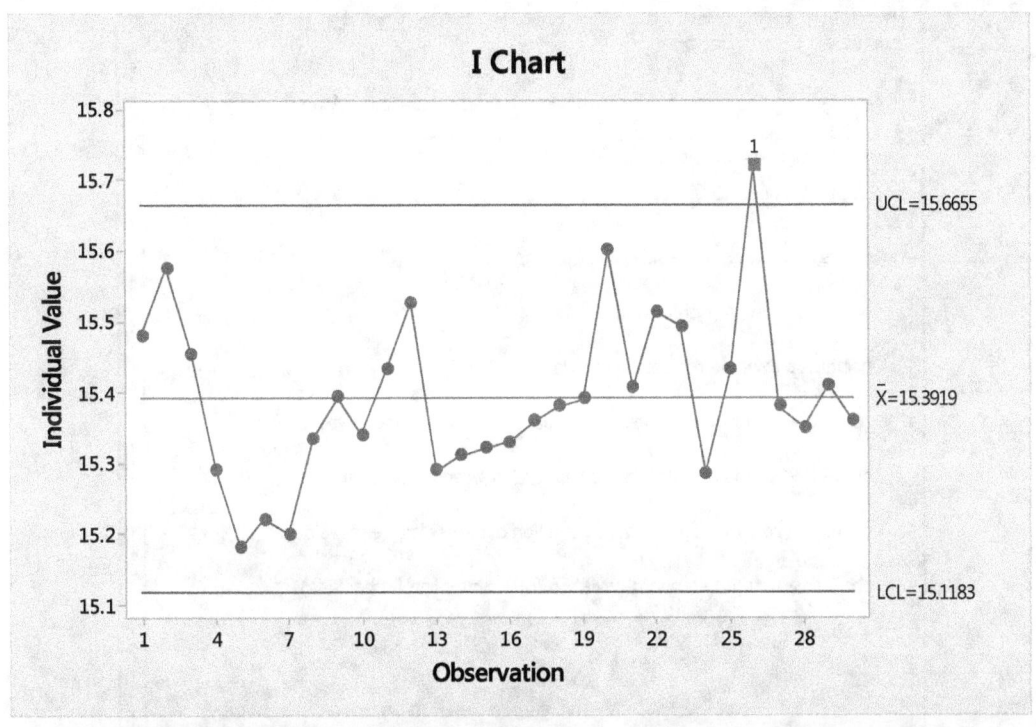

Figure 6.1: I chart example with one out-of-control point

A data point that more than three standard deviations from the centerline is one indicator for detecting special-cause variation in a process. There are additional control chart rules introduced by Dr. Lloyd S. Nelson in his April 1984 *Journal of Quality Technology* column (1984). There are eight Nelson Rules and if you're interested in using them, they can be activated in Minitab.

To activate the Nelson rules, go to **Control Charts > Variables Charts for Individuals > Individuals** and then click on "I Chart Options." Go to the "Tests" tab and place a check mark next to the test you would like to select—or simply use the drop-down menu and select "Perform all tests for special causes," as shown in Figure 6.2.

PRACTICAL STATISTICAL METHODS FOR QUALITY

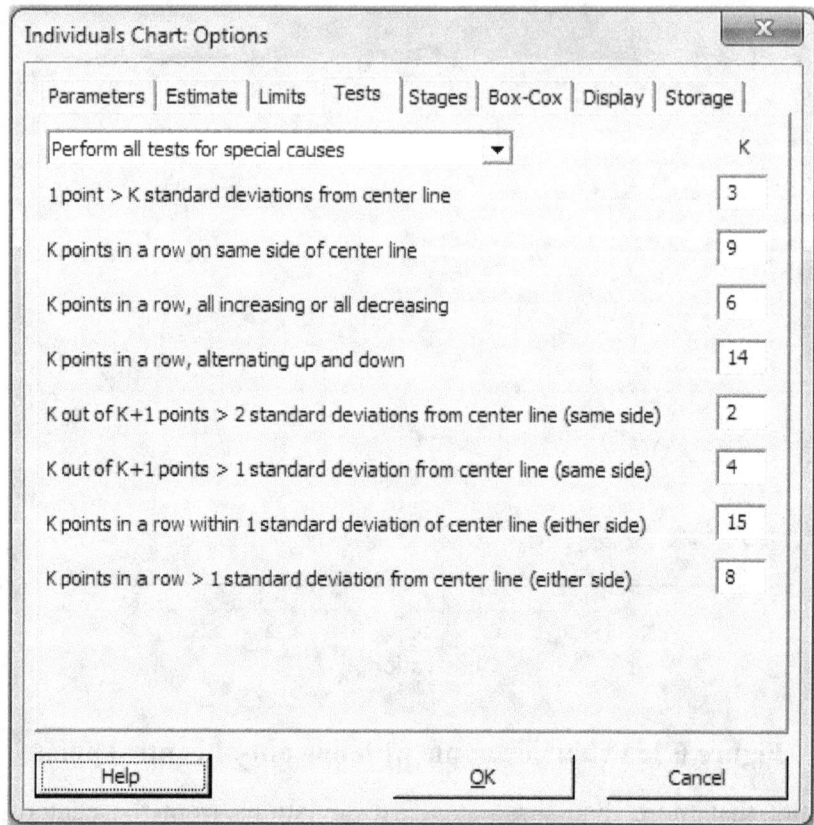

Figure 6.2: The resulting session window explains which tests failed

The session window (see Fig. 6.3) shows the tests which have failed and the out of control points are identified in the I chart as a square box with the number of the test that was failed as shown in Figure 6.4.

Test Results for I Chart of Data

TEST 1. One point more than 3.00 standard deviations from center line.
Test Failed at points: 26
TEST 3. 6 points in a row all increasing or all decreasing.
Test Failed at points: 19; 20
TEST 5. 2 out of 3 points more than 2 standard deviations from center line (on one side of CL).
Test Failed at points: 7
TEST 6. 4 out of 5 points more than 1 standard deviation from center line (on one side of CL).
Test Failed at points: 7

* WARNING * If graph is updated with new data, the results above may no longer be correct.

Figure 6.3: Session window for an I chart

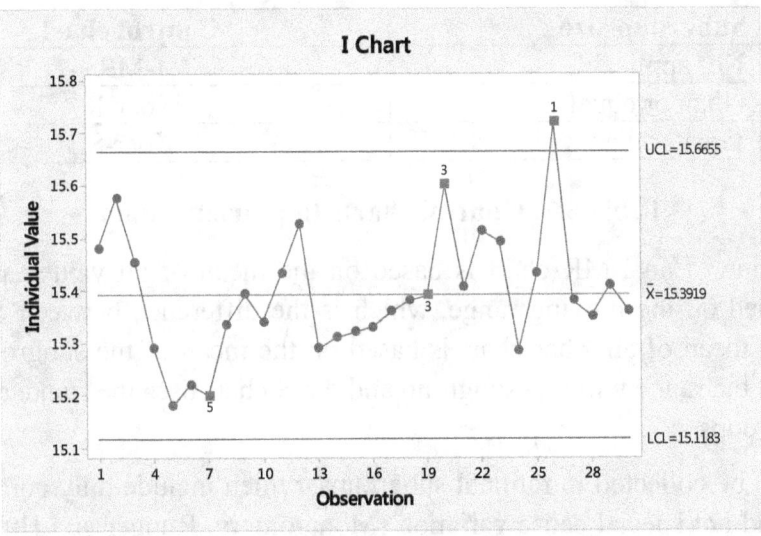

Figure 6.4: I chart with many out of control points

Wheeler warns us "As the number of detection rules increases, the likelihood of a false alarm will also increase" (Wheeler 1995 p. 139). Simply activating all of the rules is not recommended—the false positive rate goes up as each additional rule is activated. At some point the control chart will become more sensitive than it needs to be and corrective actions for special causes of variation may be implemented when only common cause is variation present.

Minitab, together with the Nelson rules, can be very helpful, but neither can replace or remove the need for the analyst's judgment when assessing a control chart. These rules can, however, assist the analyst in making the proper decision.

6.2 Selecting a Control Does not Need to be Scary

For the inexperienced, selecting a control chart can be scary and intimidating, but that does not need to be the case. The correct type of control chart should be selected based upon the data. Suppose we needed to set up a control chart for a production line producing hard candies for Halloween. Which type of control chart should we use?

Charts for Variable Data If we are dealing with measurements such as length, weight, diameter, or angle, we would use a control chart for variable data (see Table 6.2), which is also known as continuous data. The exact chart will depend upon the subgroup size. An I-MR chart is used for data that was not collected in subgroups, an Xbar-R chart is used for subgroup sizes equal to or less than 8, and an Xbar-S chart is used when the subgroup is size greater than 8.

Subgroup size	Control chart
Not applicable	I-MR
Less than or equal to 8	Xbar-R
Greater than 8	Xbar-S

Table 6.2: Control charts for variable data

The centerline of an I-MR chart is based on the mean of all values and the MR chart is based on the moving range, which is the difference between consecutive values. The mean of an Xbar chart is based on the mean of the subgroups. The R chart shows the range within a subgroup and the S chart uses the standard deviation of the subgroups.

Data should be collected in rational subgroups, which include only common cause variation and not special cause variation (Montgomery, Runger and Hubele 2001). In our example we select five hard candies produced from the same batch of raw material and measure the diameter in millimeters. We do this once very hour for 5 hours. The results are shown in Table 6.3

Subrgoup	1st sample	2nd sample	3rd sample	4th sample	5th sample
SG1	16.98	17.07	17.04	17.01	17.09
SG2	17.15	16.99	17.14	17.15	16.93
SG3	17.06	17.07	16.99	16.88	16.89
SG4	17.12	17.03	17.07	17.03	17.11
SG5	17.00	16.92	16.94	17.01	17.06

Table 6.3: Data in subgroups

We select an Xbar-R chart since we have variable data and a subgroup size of 5. Go to **Control Charts > Variables Charts for Subgroups > Xbar-R** and select "Observations for a subgroup are in one row of columns" and select the columns containing data and the subgroups. If the subgroups had all been in one column, we would have selected "All observations for a chart are in one column" and then either select the column containing the subgroup identifier or would have entered the size of the subgroup. The resulting Xbar-R chart is shown in Figure 6.5.

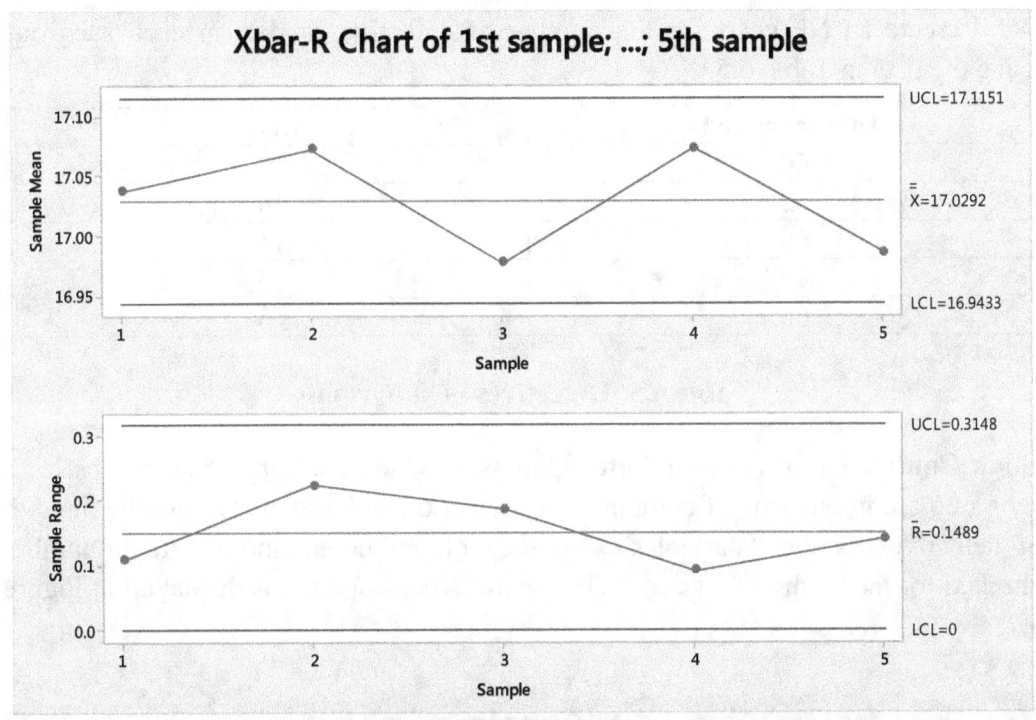

Figure 6.5: Xbar-R chart

Charts for Attribute Data Instead of measuring a dimension, we could have assessed the quality of the individual hard candies and created a control chart of attribute data (see Table 6.4). Attribute data pertains to "A characteristic or property that is apprised in terms of whether it does or does not exist (e.g. Go or NoGO) with respect to a given requirement" (Griffith 2003 p. 567).

Used for	Control chart
Proportion defective	P chart
Defective items per subgroup	NP chart
Defects per unit	U chart
Defects in subgroup	C chart

Table 6.4: Control charts for attribute data

Suppose we pulled a large sample of hard candies and found quality problems such as cracked candies, porosity, and measurement deviations. We would use the U chart for defects per unit such as one candy with two separate problems. An alternative would be to total the number of defects in the subgroup and use the C chart. But in this case, it may not make sense to count each individual defect on a candy. Instead, we could count any candy with 1 or more defects as 1 defective and use the P chart to monitor the proportion of candies defective in every subgroup.

We'll create an NP chart for the number of defective candies in each subgroup using the data in Table 6.5.

Total checked	n.OK
60	12
62	14
60	11
70	15
68	13

Table 6.5: Defectives in subgroups

Go to **Control Charts** > **Attributes Charts** > **NP** and select "Observations for a subgroup are in one row of columns" and select the column containing the number of defectives as the "Variables" and the column containing the total number checked for the "Subgroup sizes." The resulting control chart is displayed in Figure 6.7.

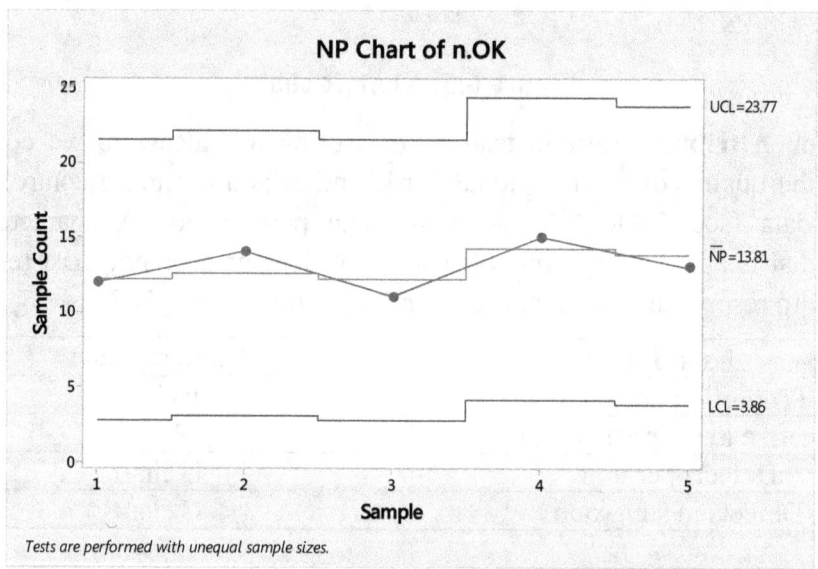

Figure 6.7: NP chart

Conclusion Although there are many types of control charts to choose from, the decision does not need to be difficult as the correct type of control chart will be determined by the type of data that results from what we decide to monitor.

CHAPTER 7

Design of Experiments

Design of Experiments is as an economical way of performing experiments; a study that requires hundreds of tests can be reduced to a manageable number while delivering useful information. The related terminology is illustrated using the example of experiments performed using a catapult. The reader is walked through the experiment to show both how to plan and conduct the experiment and how to analyze it using Minitab. A second example uses experiments performed using a paper helicopter. The paper helicopter study did not have sufficient degrees of freedom to calculate P-values; therefore, removing factors to reduce the model and increase the available degrees of freedom is covered.

In addition to describing how to analyze the experiment using Minitab, reducing variability in conducting the experiment is covered. Selecting the required resolution and interpreting main effects plots and interaction plots is described. Using the Minitab response optimizer to identify the optimal settings is explained.

7.1 Experiment for a DIY DoE Catapult

Learning to perform DoE (Design of Experiments) is much easier if there is something to practice on. Along with paper helicopters, catapults are a common DoE training aid. The biggest disadvantage of the catapult is the space required to perform the experiment and the cost of purchasing a catapult (Woody and Einwalter 1997); however, the cost problem can be eliminated by building a catapult from scratch.

Here, fractional factorial DoE using a homemade catapult will be explained. A fractional factorial does not evaluate every possible combination and catapult setting; however, it is more economical to perform than a general full factorial, which evaluates every possible combination. Another alternative could be a full factorial, which evaluates every possible combination, but only using the highest and lowest catapult settings; however, performing a full factorial may still be uneconomical

Planning the Designed Experiment: Possible Factors and Levels In DoE, each experiment performed is a run and the response variable is what is evaluated after each run. The response for the catapult experiment is the distance traveled by a projectile. The potential influences that are used in the DoE and varied between runs are the factors (Lawson and Erjavec 2001). The settings of the factors are called levels.

The catapult has 6 factors with three possible levels each. The factors are:

1. rubber band guide
2. arm stopper
3. starting point
4. rubber band
5. rubber band attachment on arm
6. projectile

The rubber band guide increases the distance the rubber band must travel and thereby stretches the rubber band. The rubber band guide can be set at one of three possible heights by moving the metal rod to the screw eye at the required height. The levels are the distance from the top of the base of the catapult to the center of the screw eye for the guide.

The arm stopper stops the catapults arm after lunch and the factors are the distance from the beginning of the support connector to the center of the screw eye for the stopper.

The starting point is the lowest point at which the catapult arm can be pushed down to prior to launching the projectile. The levels are the distances from the top of the base to the middle of the screw eyes used for the starting points.

The rubber band factors are the diameters of the rubber bands, and the projectile factors are the weight of the bags of rice used as a projectile. The final factor is the point where the rubber band is attached to the catapult arm; the three levels are the distances from the end of the arm to the attachment point.

The table below shows the factors and their possible levels are shown in Table 7.1.

Factor	First level	Second level	Third level
Rubber band guide	4 cm	9 cm	14 cm

Arm stopper	5 cm	10 cm	15 cm
Starting point	3 cm	8 cm	13 cm
Rubber band	90 mm	100 mm	130 mm
Projectile	25 g	37.5 g	50 g
Attachment on arm	14 cm	18 cm	22 cm

Table 7.1: Factors and levels

Additional levels are possible. There is enough room on the catapult to add more levels to the rubber band guide, arm stopper and starting point. There are also more rubber band sizes available and the weight of the projectiles is not infinite, but limited only by the upper limit of what the catapult can throw. For most DoE trials six factors with three levels should be sufficient. This results in 3^6 possible combinations. That means 729 combinations. Adding an extra level to each factor would result in 4,096 combinations and a fifth level would result in 15,625 combinations. Doubling the number of levels to six would result in 46,656 different combinations.

The catapult may be large enough to accommodate six levels for each of the six possible factors; however, DoE would be needed to find the optimal settings without running all possible combinations.

The DoE Experiment I had to put the catapult to use after finishing with the assembly. The first experiment performed using the catapult was a 2^3 full factorial with no replicates. This means that three factors were evaluated, each at two levels, and each treatment was run only one time. To create a DoE worksheet, go to **DOE > Factorial > Create Factorial Design** and select "2-level factor (default generators)" under "Type of Design" and select 3 as the "Number of factors" using the dropdown menu. Click on **Designs** and select Full factorial. Run the experiment and enter the results into Minitab. Then go to **DOE > Factorial > Analyze Factorial Design.**

Alternatively, the factors and levels for the experiments well as the results shown in Table 7.2 can be copied into a new Minitab worksheet. Go to **DOE > Factorial > Analyze Factorial Design** and Minitab will ask for the factors, levels, and response.

Projectile	Rubber band	Starting point	Response
10	90	3	500.7
10	90	13	418.3
10	130	3	374.3
10	130	13	285

20	90	3	512
20	90	13	398.7
20	130	3	334.3
20	130	13	261.3

Table 7.2: Factors, levels, and results

The resulting Minitab worksheet showed asterisks in place of P-values; this is an indication that there was not enough variability in the study. More replicates may have been necessary. Figure 7.1 shows a Pareto chart of effects; only the rubber band and starting pints were statistically significant.

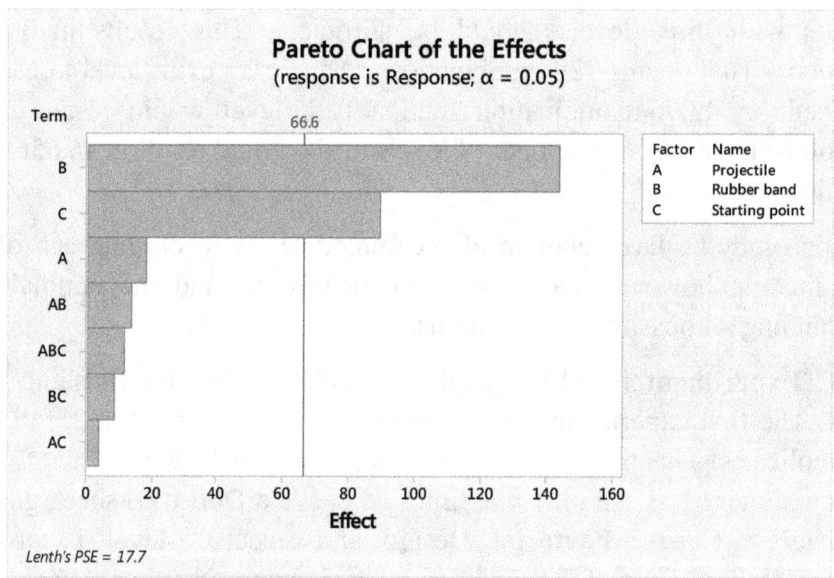

Figure 7.1: Pareto chart of effects

Each run was performed at a high and low value for the factors. Run order was determined at random to ensure randomization. This was essential to ensure that the results were indeed the results of the factors and levels evaluated, and not changes in the system as the testing progressed. For example, the rubber bands used may stretch during testing. Randomization helps to ensure the test results of such uncontrollable factors are spread across the test result, and Minitab Statistical Software's DoE tools provide a randomized run order by default.

The experiment was performed the runs in the order determined by the software and recorded the results. Next, generate a main effects plot and an interaction plot for the response variable, distance traveled by the projectile by going to **DOE >**

Factorial > Factorial Plots. The main effects plot is shown in Figure 7.2 and the interaction plot is shown in Figure 7.3.

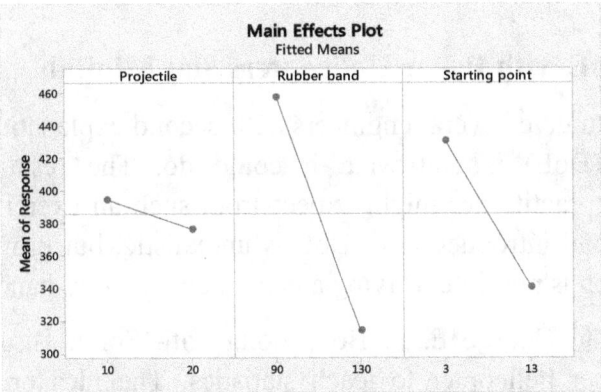

Figure 7.2: Main effects plot

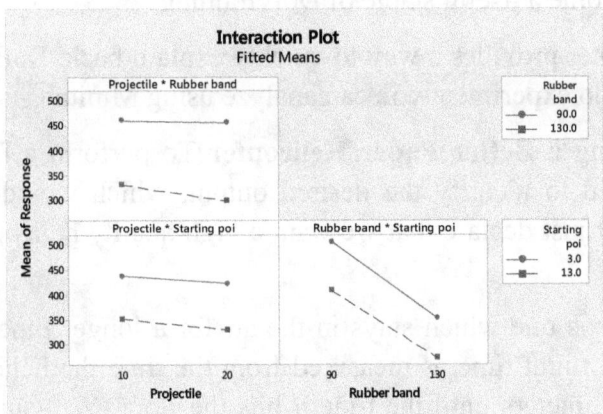

Figure 7.3: Interaction plot

The results indicate that the interactions were not significant. However, the analysis results shown in the main effects plot indicate a large difference between the high and low settings for both rubber band and starting point. This makes sense, since the smaller rubber band should provide more force than the larger rubber band. The lower starting point for the catapult arm results in a greater distance of travel between the release point of the arm and the stopping point where the arm releases the projectile.

The effect of the projectile weight was not as important as the other factors. This may be due to the very light weight of the projectiles. The higher setting was twice the weight of the low setting; however, the lower setting was only the equivalent of approximately 4 quarters. Maybe a difference of a dollar's worth of quarters is too little to result in a larger main effect for distance traveled? This could also be investigated using the catapult and Minitab.

7.2 Teaching DoE with Paper Helicopters and Minitab

I once attempted to give several engineers a 30-second explanation of what Design of Experiments (DoE) is and what it could do. The results were what an experienced DoE practitioner might expect from such an exercise: a total failure. Perhaps a 30-second introduction to DoE is unrealistic, but providing a short and concise explanation is possible. Having a paper helicopter on hand helps.

The late statistician George E. P. Box, along with Soren Bisgaard and Conrad Fung, used a paper helicopter to teach statistics. The idea originated with Kip Rogers of Digital Equipment (Box 1992) and is useful for demonstrating fractional factorial designs. Decades after Box, Bisgaard and Fung's publication, the DoE helicopter has become a useful staple of DoE training.

The paper helicopter provides a way to quickly explain basic DoE concepts. It also offers an easy-to-do experiment you can analyze using Minitab.

The Goal: Making a Better Paper Helicopter To perform a DoE with a paper helicopter we need to identify the desired output, which would be our response variable. We can't just declare that we want a high quality helicopter; quality must be clearly defined.

A good helicopter is one which stays in the air for a longer time, so the response variable would be flight time as measured from the time the helicopter is dropped from a height of 2 meters until the time it hits the floor. Without defining the test conditions, it could be possible that sample helicopters would be dropped from different heights, in which case our DoE results would be not be valid.

Test factors that influence flight time must also be identified. For the helicopter experiment, the factors are paper type, rotor length, leg length, leg width and paper clip (see Table 7.3). The helicopter experiment levels are varied by using two different types of paper, using longer or shorter leg and rotor lengths and adding or removing a paper clip.

Factor	Low setting (-)	High setting (+)	Factor
Paper type	Light	Heavy	Paper type
Rotor length	7.5 cm	8.5 cm	Rotor length
Leg length	7.5 cm	12.0 cm	Leg length
Leg width	3.2 cm	5.0 cm	Leg width
Paper clip on leg	No	Yes	Paper clip on leg

Table 7.3: Helicopter factors

Designing the Experiment Statisticians and Six Sigma black belts should know how to set up and perform the calculations in a designed experiment by hand; however, computer programs make DoE a much simpler task, particularly for people who need to perform experiments only occasionally.

To create a fractional factorial design in Minitab Statistical Software, go to **DoE > Factorial > Create Factorial Design** and select the desired design. For this experiment, we will use a 2-level factorial which can handle from two to fifteen different factors. To select the desired design in Minitab, select 5 for the "Number of factors," then click "Designs" to select the desired design and resolution level.

Resolution is the degree to which effects are aliased with other effects. In other words, aliased effects are mixed together and can't be estimated separately. This can also be referred to as confounding (Durivage 2016), and it results from not testing every possible combination of factors. This is a disadvantage of a fractional factorial design; however, not testing every possible combination can be a significant advantage in time and expense over a full factorial design.

If you're not sure what resolution you should use, click on "Display Available Design" to see a list of designs and resolutions.

In the quality realm, we typically use three levels of resolution: resolution III, IV and V. There is no confounding of main effects with each other in these three resolution types; however, in a resolution III design, main effects will be confounded with 2-factor interactions. Resolution IV designs do not have 2-factor confounding with main effects, but 2-factor interactions are aliased with other 2-factor interactions, and main effects are confounded with 3-factor interactions.

We try to use resolution IV designs instead of resolution III designs when possible because they have less aliasing, but still require fewer experimental runs than higher resolution experiments.

Resolution V designs have the added advantage that no 2-factor effects are confounded with other 2-factor effects; however, 2-factor effects are aliased with 3-factor effects, and main effects are aliased with 4-factor effects.

The confounding problem can be eliminated by performing a full factorial design; however, this requires more experimental runs, which might be prohibitive in terms of both time and money.

Looking at "Display Available Designs" in Minitab, we can conduct a fractional factorial experiment using either a resolution III or a resolution V design for the 5 factor helicopter experiment. A resolution III design would only need 8 runs, but the resolution V design that requires 16 test runs is the better option. Click on "Designs" and select the desired design.

As you set up the experiment, Minitab also asks for the number of blocks. Blocks are simply homogenous groupings of measurements that can be used to account for variation (Box, Hunter and Hunter 2005). The default value is one; ideally, everything is homogenous.

The helicopter experiment will be set up so that there is only one experimental block: each type of paper will come from the same source; the helicopters will all be built by the same person using the same scissors and ruler. If we had a paper clip shortage that forced us to use paper clips from two manufacturers, then we would need blocks to account for potential variation in the paper clips. Fortunately, this is not the case.

After you select your design, click the "Factors" button to enter the names and levels of the variables in your experiment. To change the name of a factor, simply type the name of the factor over the letter in the name field. The factor settings can also be renamed by replacing the default values of -1 and 1 with the actual factor levels.

When you've completed the dialog box, Minitab creates the experimental design and displays it in a Minitab worksheet (see Figure 7.4). The session window above the worksheet provides a description of the selected design with the resulting alias structure (see Fig. 7.5).

↓	C1	C2	C3	C4	C5-T	C6	C7	C8	C9-T	C10
	StdOrder	RunOrder	CenterPt	Blocks	Paper type	Rotor length	Leg length	Leg width	Paper clip on leg	
1	11	1	1	1	Light	8.5	7.5	5.0	Yes	
2	3	2	1	1	Light	8.5	7.5	3.2	No	
3	2	3	1	1	Heavy	7.5	7.5	3.2	No	
4	7	4	1	1	Light	8.5	12.0	3.2	Yes	
5	16	5	1	1	Heavy	8.5	12.0	5.0	Yes	
6	13	6	1	1	Light	7.5	12.0	5.0	Yes	
7	14	7	1	1	Heavy	7.5	12.0	5.0	No	
8	10	8	1	1	Heavy	7.5	7.5	5.0	Yes	
9	9	9	1	1	Light	7.5	7.5	5.0	No	
10	4	10	1	1	Heavy	8.5	7.5	3.2	Yes	
11	12	11	1	1	Heavy	8.5	7.5	5.0	No	
12	15	12	1	1	Light	8.5	12.0	5.0	No	
13	6	13	1	1	Heavy	7.5	12.0	3.2	Yes	
14	1	14	1	1	Light	7.5	7.5	3.2	Yes	
15	8	15	1	1	Heavy	8.5	12.0	3.2	No	
16	5	16	1	1	Light	7.5	12.0	3.2	No	
17										

Figure 7.4: Minitab worksheet

Fractional Factorial Design

Design Summary

Factors:	5	Base Design:	5; 16	Resolution:	V
Runs:	16	Replicates:	1	Fraction:	1/2
Blocks:	1	Center pts (total):	0		

Design Generators: E = ABCD

Alias Structure

I + ABCDE
A + BCDE
B + ACDE
C + ABDE
D + ABCE
E + ABCD
AB + CDE
AC + BDE
AD + BCE
AE + BCD
BC + ADE
BD + ACE
BE + ACD
CD + ABE
CE + ABD
DE + ABC

Figure 7.5: Session window with alias structure

In the resulting Minitab worksheet shown above, the experimental results are entered into column C10. We can name the column "Flight time" because that is our experimental response variable.

A randomized run order is provided in the "RunOrder" column. Without randomization there is a risk that the experimental results will reflect unknown changes in the test system over time. For example, in the helicopter experiment, the scissors may become dull over time, resulting in slightly different cuts as each new helicopter is prepared.

Minitab's default setting for a designed experiment is one replicate. If you observe a lot of variation in the process or the resulting measurements, you can use **Stat** > **DoE** > **Modify Design** to add replicates to your design. Suppose the person making the helicopters had difficulty cutting a straight line so all edges are not uniform; the differences in results may reflect this variation. Replicating runs minimizes the effects of this kind of unanticipated variation.

Gathering the Experimental Data Variability can have a major impact on experimental results, so take steps to reduce the variability. Have the same person make all of the helicopters using the same scissors and ruler. Drop the helicopters from a height of 2 meters, and identify the drop point clearly to ensure consistency. A higher or lower starting point would affect flight time, and this could throw off the results. The helicopters must also be held and released the same way, or variation in our data might be the effect of the release method and not the design of the helicopter.

Either run the helicopter experiment yourself and enter the data into Minitab, or copy the results from Table 7.4 into Minitab and go to **DoE > Factorial > Analyze Factorial Design** and Minitab will ask for the factors, levels, and response.

Paper type	Rotor length	Leg length	Leg width	Paper clip on leg	Flight time
1	7.5	12	2	1	1.56
2	8.5	12	3	2	1.65
1	8.5	12	3	1	1.87
2	7.5	12	2	2	1.27
2	8.5	7.5	3	1	1.76
2	8.5	7.5	2	2	1.64
1	8.5	7.5	2	1	2.3
1	7.5	12	3	2	1.61
1	7.5	7.5	3	1	2.1
2	7.5	7.5	2	1	1.58
2	7.5	12	3	1	1.54
1	7.5	7.5	2	2	1.98
1	8.5	7.5	3	2	1.99
2	8.5	12	2	1	1.62
2	7.5	7.5	3	2	1.57
1	8.5	12	2	2	1.8

Table 7.4: Helicopter experiment results

Analyzing the Data After running the experiment and entering the collected data in the Minitab worksheet, select **DoE > Factorial > Analyze Factorial Design**. Significant factors are those that influence the response as they changed from one setting to another. When you click OK, Minitab provides a Pareto chart of effects (see Fig. 7.6), which makes it very easy to identify significant factors as well as an ANOVA table (See Fig. 7.7).

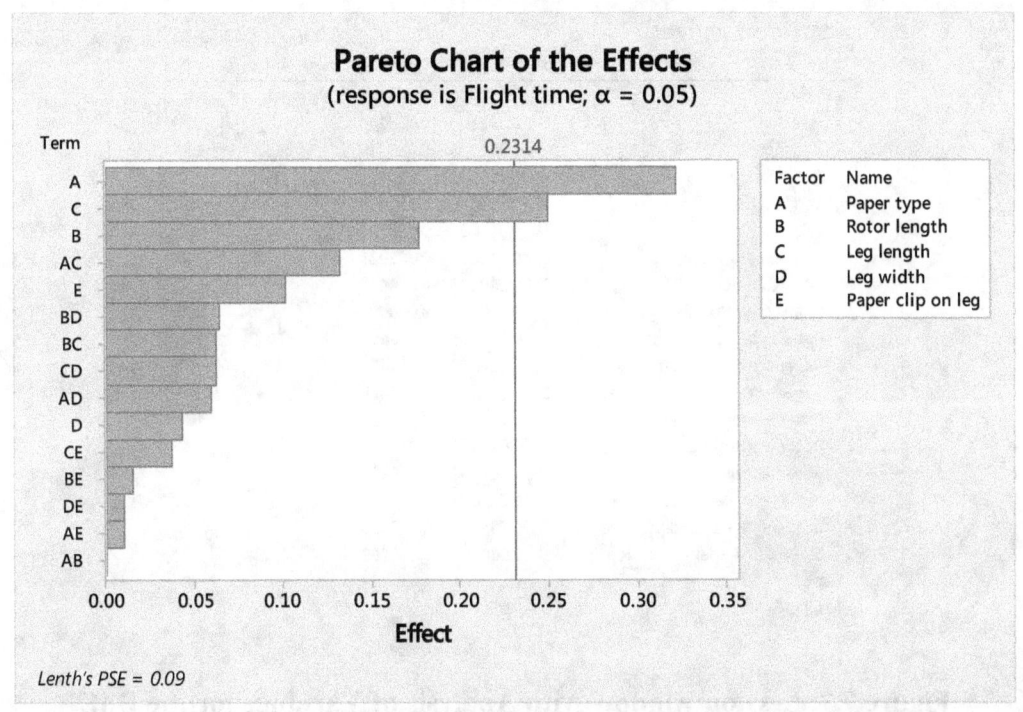

Figure 7.6: Pareto chart of effects

In an ANOVA table, those factors with a P-value less than 0.05 are statistically significant. However, the ANOVA table for this model doesn't include any P-values!

Analysis of Variance

Source	DF	Adj SS	Adj MS	F-Value	P-Value
Model	15	0.981400	0.065427	*	*
Linear	5	0.841300	0.168260	*	*
Paper type	1	0.416025	0.416025	*	*
Rotor length	1	0.126025	0.126025	*	*
Leg length	1	0.250000	0.250000	*	*
Leg width	1	0.007225	0.007225	*	*
Paper clip on leg	1	0.042025	0.042025	*	*
2-Way Interactions	10	0.140100	0.014010	*	*
Paper type*Rotor length	1	0.000000	0.000000	*	*
Paper type*Leg length	1	0.070225	0.070225	*	*
Paper type*Leg width	1	0.014400	0.014400	*	*
Paper type*Paper clip on leg	1	0.000400	0.000400	*	*
Rotor length*Leg length	1	0.015625	0.015625	*	*
Rotor length*Leg width	1	0.016900	0.016900	*	*
Rotor length*Paper clip on leg	1	0.000900	0.000900	*	*
Leg length*Leg width	1	0.015625	0.015625	*	*
Leg length*Paper clip on leg	1	0.005625	0.005625	*	*
Leg width*Paper clip on leg	1	0.000400	0.000400	*	*
Error	0	*	*		
Total	15	0.981400			

Figure 7.7: Session window with Analysis of Variance for the DoE

This is because with all of our factors included in the model, we have no degrees of freedom left for Error, and you need at least 1 degree of freedom to calculate P-values. But while we can't accept this model based on the ANOVA results, we can use the normal plot or Pareto chart to identify factors and interactions that are not significant.

At this point, the experimenter would typically begin eliminating these factors, rerunning the analysis until only significant factors and interactions are left. This is usually referred to as "reducing the model." As factors are removed from the model, additional degrees of freedom become available for the calculation of P-values. The number of models you need to evaluate depends on the number of factors in your analysis.

With the stepwise DoE tool in Minitab 17, reducing the model is a one-step process. To use this feature, return to the "Analyze Factorial Design" dialog box, select C10 Flight time as the "Response, then press the "Stepwise" button.

The stepwise regression feature makes it simple and fast to select the optimal model for your data by automatically removing factors to find the model that best fits your data. You can choose from three stepwise analysis methods: Stepwise, Forward selection, and Backward elimination. In Backward elimination, all factors are included in the initial analysis, and then non-significant factors are removed one-by-one. Regardless of the stepwise method you use, the model Minitab selects contains the same significant factors shown in Figure 7.8.

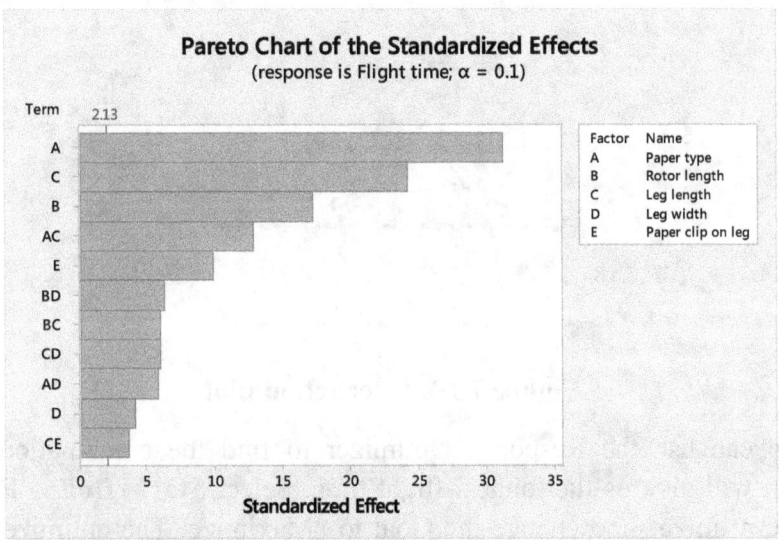

Figure 7.8: Pareto chart of standardized effects

To help you interpret your results, Minitab can also provide main effects and interaction plots. Select **DoE** > **Factorial** > **Factorial Plots.** Since we have already analyzed the results, Minitab automatically selects the factors used in our model. Clicking OK gives us plots of the significant main effects and interactions. The main effects plot in Figure 7.9 shows the results of changing from one setting to another for each factor.

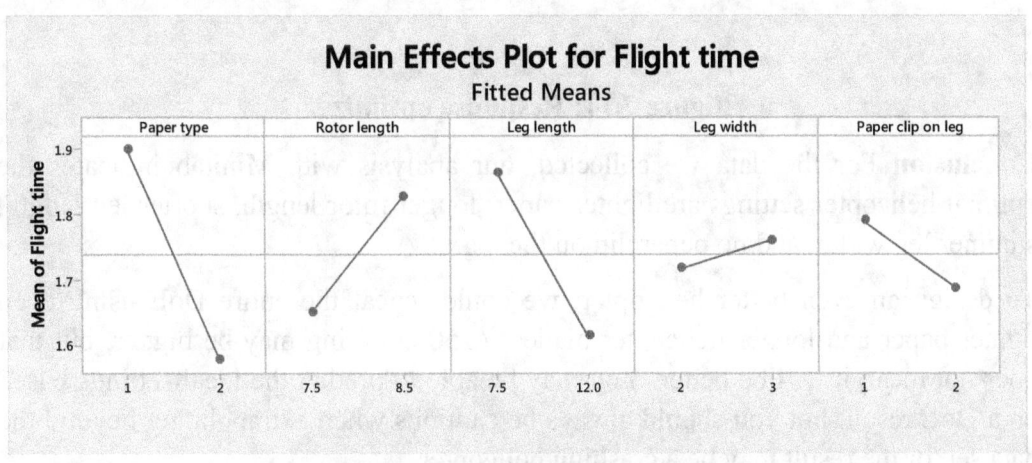

Figure 7.9: Main effects plot

The interaction plot in Figure 7.10 shows the interactions between the factors.

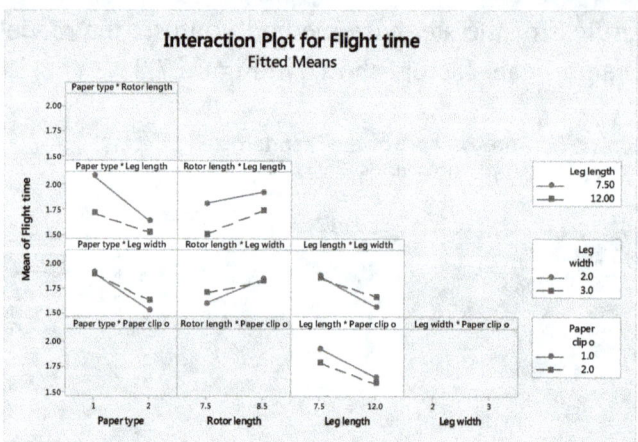

Figure 7.10: Interaction plot

Finally, we can use the Response Optimizer to find the combination of factor settings that will give us the longest flight time. Select **Stat** > **DoE** > **Factorial** > **Response Optimizer** and change the Goal to "Maximize. The optimizer produces the graph in Figure 7.11 showing the optimal factor settings and the predicted response for helicopters made with those settings.

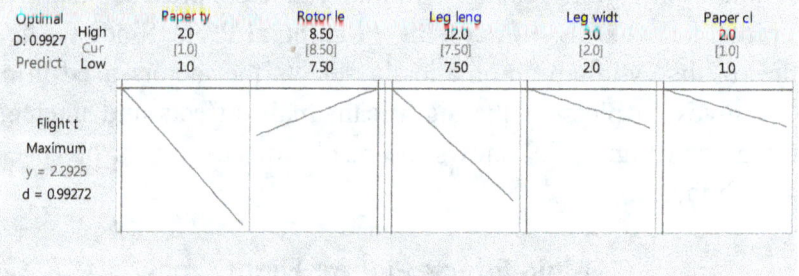

Figure 7.11: Response optimizer

Conclusion For the data we collected, our analysis with Minitab indicates the optimal helicopter settings are lighter paper, longer rotor length, shorter leg length, slimmer leg width, and no paperclip on the leg.

To design an even better helicopter, we could repeat the entire DoE using even lighter paper and longer helicopter blades. A 50 cm wing may be bigger, but that does not mean it will be better. You may be able to predict the ideal settings based on a DoE result, but you should always be cautious when extrapolating beyond the data set, or the result may be a crashing helicopter.

CHAPTER 8

Conclusion

Various statistical methods such as a two-sample t-test, regression analysis and test of two portions are performed. A mean and standard deviation is also found by using the Display Descriptive Statistics function in Minitab and the data is plotted in an individual value chart. However, the main lesson is how to properly perform a statistical test such as selecting the variable that matters and not simply the data that is easily available. Statistics uses math, but it is not about the math, statistics is performed as a way to gain new knowledge or interpret data in a way that permits the correct decision to be made.

This chapter concludes by reiterating why statistics matter and reminds readers that proper test selection is essential to getting results that help to make the correct decision. Statistics is not about simply determining if there is a statistically significant difference between two data sets; the test is performed to gain insights that can be used for better decision making.

8.1 Flight of the Chickens: A Minitab Bedtime Story

Once upon a time there was a farm with over a thousand chickens, two pigs, and a cow (see Figure 8.1). The chickens were well treated, but there were a few rabble rousers amongst them who got them worked up. These chickens looked almost like other chickens, but they were evil chickens.

PRACTICAL STATISTICAL METHODS FOR QUALITY

Figure 8.1: Animals on the farm © Vanessa Friese. Used with permission

Hidden among the good chickens and the evil chickens was Sid. Sid was not like other chickens. He was a secret spy for The Swan of the Lahn who ruled Wetzlar. Sid was also a duck. Yes, a duck. A duck disguised as a chicken. The duck spied for the Swan of the Lahn, who was concerned with the presence of all the evil chickens. Sid knew who the evil chickens were and sent regular reports on their activities.

One stormy and dark night an evil chicken snuck out with an enormous basket of beautiful hand-painted eggs to throw at the two pigs and the cow. Sid snuck out into the pouring rain and took a sample of 18 eggs (see Table 8.1). The intrepid duck he knew that a previous study of 157 eggs showed that the mean of the eggs was 57.079 grams with a standard deviation of 2.30 grams (Atwood 1925). Sid was determined to find out if his current samples had a statically significant difference when compared to the mean of the previous study.

We will need to use summarized data since we only have actual values for the sample from the study and not the full data set. Using the data in Table 8.1, go to **Stat > Basic Statistics > Display Descriptive Statistics** and select the column containing the data as the "Variable." Click on "Graphs" and select Individual value plot to view a graph of the data. Click OK twice and Minitab will create an individual value plot of the data (see Fig. 8.2) and the mean and standard deviation will appear in the session window with the rest of the descriptive statistics as shown in Figure 8.3.

Eggs
61.5
58.6
56.6
57.9
59.8
57.3
56.9
57.4
56.2
55.2
56.1
60.2
56.3
50.9
60.5
54.9
57.6
57.7

Table 8.1: Egg weights

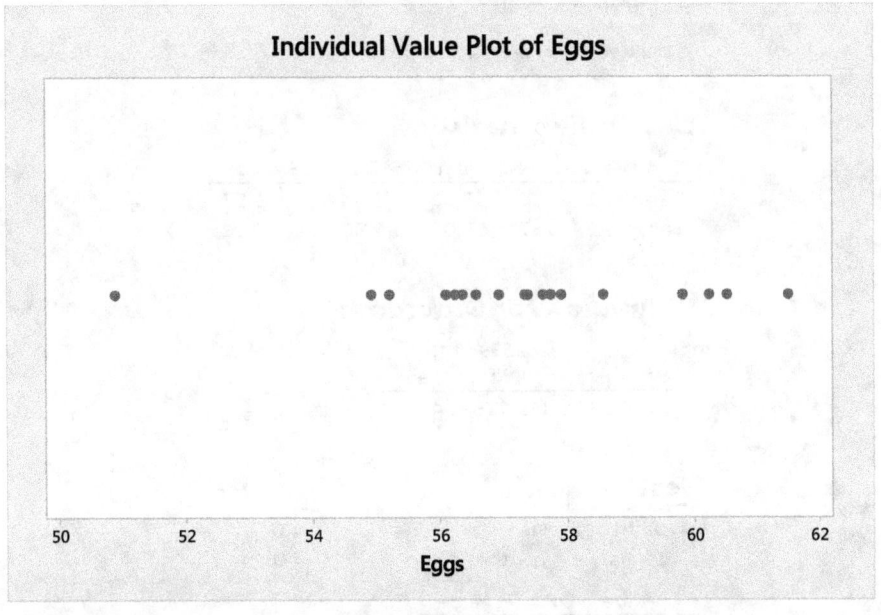

Figure 8.2: Individual value plot of eggs

Descriptive Statistics: Eggs

Statistics

Variable	N	N*	Mean	SE Mean	StDev	Minimum	Q1	Median	Q3	Maximum
Eggs	18	0	57.315	0.575	2.439	50.851	56.200	57.355	58.874	61.495

Figure 8.3.: Session window for descriptive statistics for eggs

We can see that the sample mean is 57.315 and the standard deviation is 2.439 so now we can perform a 2 sample t-test to compare the means by going to **Stat > Basic Statistics > 2-Sample t** and selecting Summarized data in the drop down menu. Enter the sample size of 18, sample mean of 57.315 and standard deviation of 2.439 under Sample 1 and enter the sample size of 157, mean of 57.079, and the population standard deviation of 2.30 under Sample 2. Then click OK and the results will appear in the session window as shown in Figure 8.4.

Two-Sample T-Test and CI

Method

μ_1: mean of Sample 1
μ_2: mean of Sample 2
Difference: $\mu_1 - \mu_2$

Equal variances are not assumed for this analysis.

Descriptive Statistics

Sample	N	Mean	StDev	SE Mean
Sample 1	18	57.31	2.44	0.57
Sample 2	157	57.08	2.30	0.18

Estimation for Difference

Difference	95% CI for Difference
0.236	(-1.023; 1.495)

Test

Null hypothesis $H_0: \mu_1 - \mu_2 = 0$
Alternative hypothesis $H_1: \mu_1 - \mu_2 \neq 0$

T-Value	DF	P-Value
0.39	20	0.700

Figure 8.4: Session window for a Two-Sample Test

The p-value is greater than 0.05 so we can conclude there is no statically significant difference in the means. Unfortunately, Sid made a critical mistake. His statistics were correct, but he asked the wrong question. His question was "Is the mean of the second sample different than the mean of the first sample with an alpha of 0.05?" What he should have asked was "What will happen if the pigs and cow get hit by eggs?" The first step in an analysis is to ask the right question. The weight of the eggs were irrelevant; the consequences of the pigs and cow being pummeled with eggs are what mattered. Management, in this case The Swan of the Lahn (see Figure 8.5), reading such a report would conclude that the process has not changed. But, the correct conclusion would have been "trouble may be brewing."

The cow simply ate the eggs. But the pigs rampaged and terrorized the poor chickens that night. By midnight, the muddy fields were full of pig prints and feathers were ruffled in the chicken coop. One chicken, an evil chicken, demanded of the others "How can we live like this? The evil chickens convinced the other chickens they would all be happier if they moved to the high walled village of Wetzlar on the side of the Lahn River. The chickens began to march into the stormy night.

The chickens marched through the night and arrived at Wetzlar on the Lahn as the sun came up. "Let us in!" demanded the chickens." No" said the Swan.

Figure 8.5: The Swan of the Lahn © Vanessa Friese. Used with permission

The chickens spent the day trying to force open the gates of Wezlar while one chicken snuck off to meet with a goose known for dealing in antiques such as lamps, chairs, and main battle tanks. The chicken returned by early evening with a slightly used T-55 tank as shown in Figure 8.6.

Figure 8.6: Chicken in a T-55 tank © Vanessa Friese. Used with permission

Sid knew he must do something, so he looked up the amount of fuel used for the distance driven for 47 T-55s (see Table 8.2) and performed a regression analysis to determine how far this one could go if it had full fuel tanks.

Observation	Fuel	Distance	Observation	Fuel	Distance
1	610.6	655.0	26	640.4	694.8
2	620.0	665.6	27	641.0	696.2
3	622.6	668.0	28	641.1	696.6
4	624.4	670.4	29	641.4	696.6
5	625.8	671.8	30	642.0	698.0
6	626.3	675.6	31	644.9	698.2
7	626.6	681.9	32	645.6	699.3
8	627.7	682.3	33	645.7	699.3
9	628.7	682.3	34	645.9	699.4
10	629.3	683.1	35	648.6	702.5
11	629.3	683.3	36	649.0	704.3
12	629.7	683.8	37	649.2	704.6
13	631.1	685.6	38	649.2	706.0
14	633.5	687.5	39	649.6	709.5
15	634.4	688.5	40	649.6	711.2
16	634.8	688.7	41	651.7	715.0
17	635.5	689.6	42	652.0	716.9
18	636.3	690.4	43	652.2	717.4
19	636.9	691.4	44	653.1	723.8
20	637.8	691.9	45	654.0	725.5
21	638.0	692.8	46	656.8	728.0

22	638.1	693.9	47	659.2	729.9
23	638.3	693.9	18	659.2	730.6
24	638.3	694.1			

Table 8.2: Distance traveled

Go to **Stat > Regression > Fit Regression Model** and select Distance as the "Response" and Fuel as the "Continuous predictor." Then click on "Graphs" and select "Four in one." We can see that there is a statistically significant relationship between fuel used and distance traveled (see Figure 8.7). The amount of fuel used explains 95.28% of the variability in distance traveled. There seems to be something odd with the order of the data as seen in residual plots graph in Figure 8.8 and the session window shows us there are three unusual values, two of which have large residuals. This is an indication that our data is not perfect for a regression analysis; however, it would not matter here as the real question should have been "Can a T-55 round penetrate the gates of Weztlar?"

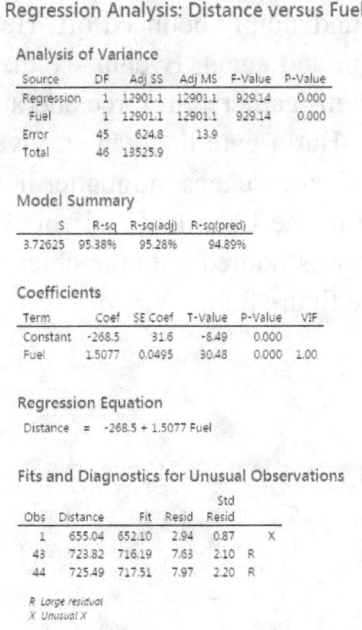

Figure 8.7: Session window for regression analysis

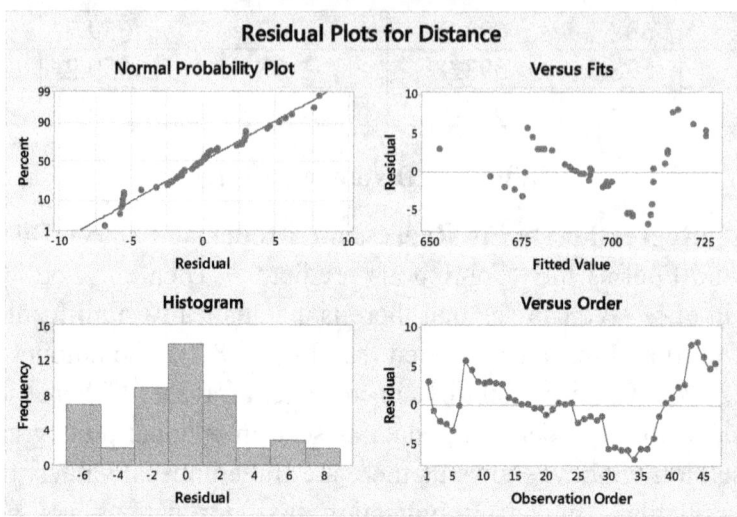

Figure 8.8: Residuals plots

The chicken with the tank huffed and puffed and fired the main gun directly at the gates of Wetzlar, but the round simply bounced off. He fired again and again, but the rounds bounced off again and again. Eventually the T-55 broke down as they are known to do so the chickens gathered in force and attempted to knock the gates down by running into them. But a gate that can survive a tank's main gun round will not budge when rammed by chickens, no matter how determined the chickens are. By this time The Swan of the Lahn had had enough so boiling chicken soup with noodles and vegetables was poured onto the chickens. This was too much for the chickens so they fled (see figure 8.9).

Figure 8.9: Chickens fleeing Wetzlar © Vanessa Friese. Used with permission

Unfortunately, the road they had followed had washed out in the heavy rains so the only route home was through the Bird Mountains. The misnamed Bird Mountains. They should have been called Hungry Foxes Everywhere Mountains. The chickens fled into the forests of the Bird Mountains.

The evil chickens knew of the foxes so they let the other chickens lead so that they would encounter the foxes first. The evil chickens failed to consider that foxes are, as they say, sly as foxes. The foxes of the misnamed Bird Mountains waited till the chickens were well into their range and then went after those in the rear; the evil chickens. Evil chickens taste like chicken and the foxes feasted (see Figure 8.10).

Figure 8.10: A well-fed fox © Vanessa Friese. Used with permission

Sid suspected the evil chickens had been decimated so he did a survey upon returning to the farm. Originaly, 647 out of the population of 1,541 of the chickens were evil so he randomly sampled 175 chickens and found only 22 of the chickens were evil. Sid wanted to know if the new proportion of evil chickens was less than the older portion so he did a one-tailed two proportion test.

Go to **Stat** > **Basic Statistics** > **2 Proportions** and select "Summarized data" in the drop down menu. Enter 22 for the "Number of events" and 175 for the "Number of trials" under "Sample 1" and enter 647 for the number of events and 1,541 for the number of trials under "Sample 2." Click on "Options" and select "Difference > hypothesized difference" and click OK twice. The resulting p-value (see Fig. 8.11) is less than 0.05 so Sid can conclude there is a statically significant difference in the samples.

Test and CI for Two Proportions

Method

p_1: proportion where Sample 1 = Event
p_2: proportion where Sample 2 = Event
Difference: $p_1 - p_2$

Descriptive Statistics

Sample	N	Event	Sample p
Sample 1	175	22	0.125714
Sample 2	1541	647	0.419857

Estimation for Difference

Difference	95% CI for Difference
-0.294143	(-0.349096; -0.239190)

CI based on normal approximation

Test

Null hypothesis H_0: $p_1 - p_2 = 0$
Alternative hypothesis H_1: $p_1 - p_2 \neq 0$

Method	Z-Value	P-Value
Normal approximation	-10.49	0.000
Fisher's exact		0.000

Figure 8.11: Session window for a two proportion test

After returning home, the chickens were confused. Just days earlier all was well and suddenly they had found themselves in such an adventure. The evil chickens were not confused, they had instigated it all. But, they were understandably upset with how things had ended and they began to argue and blame each other for the failure. Both recriminations and feathers flew.

Evil chickens started turning each other into the farmer which resulted in a weight gain for the farmer and an even greater reduction in the number of evil chickens. But this was not enough to eliminate them so Sid arranged a few "accidents" for the remaining evil chickens. The pigs eventually forgave the chickens for the egg throwing and the remaining chickens lived happily ever after. The cow spent the rest of her life hoping for another dinner of eggs and as for Sid, his next assignment was the infiltration of a rabbit den. How a duck disguised himself as a rabbit is a tale for another time (see Figure 8.12).

Figure 8.12: Duck hiding amongst rabbits © Vanessa Friese. Used with permission

There is a moral to the bedtime story: If you need help with statistics, call a statistician, not a duck.

8.2 Adventure at Sea with Hypothesis Testing of Two Samples

A strong breeze blew from the south west as the ship plied through the choppy seas with the deck awash in blood. Actually, upon further inspection, spilled pomegranate juice washed across the deck from a dropped cup. "Opps," said the old pirate who had dropped it in his haste after spotting a merchantman in the distance.

A merchantman low in the water; a sure sign of cargo or plunder, depending upon one's perspective. "Leander, turn us towards her and run her down," cried the old pirate who then continued softly with "while I mop up this spill."

Figure 8.12: Pirates © Vanessa Friese. Used with permission

The pirate ship HMS (His Moron's Ship) Las Vegas II (We don't talk about what happened to the original HMS Las Vegas and Captain Marco; see Book VI of Plato's Republic for a full accounting or the graphic rendering by Hieronymus Bosch) was a terrifying sight to behold; painted white with large wings hanging over the sides (they doubled as planks for walking unwanted prisoners and a place to dry laundry) and a swan's head as a figurehead on the bow. Now one may wonder "How terrifying can a swan be?" Anybody who wonders has never encountered an angry swan. And also, the swan's head figurehead looked angry. Angry like only a swan could be.

IMPROVING PRODUCTS, SERVICES AND PROCESSES

Figure 8.13: The pirate ship © Vanessa Friese. Used with permission

With a topgallant breeze to the rear, the HMS Las Vegas closed quickly on the unsuspecting merchantman. Upon closing the distance, the merchantman realized they were being pursued and threw up extra sails to carry them to the safety of the port of Safeharbour. But it was not enough and upon closing, Leander observed "That ship is crewed by raccoons."

Figure 8.14: A raccoon © Vanessa Friese. Used with permission

The crew of the raccoon ship consisted of 47 officer raccoons and 152 enlisted raccoons. The officers have a mean weight of 26.04 kilograms and a standard deviation of 1.16. The enlisted raccoons have a mean weight of 24.91 kilograms and a standard deviation of 1.89. Suppose the pirates wanted to know if there was a statistically significant difference in the weights. They would open Minitab and go to Stat > Basic Statistics > 2-Sample t and change the dropdown to "Summarized data." The sample size, mean, and standard deviation would be entered in the window shown in Figure 8.15.

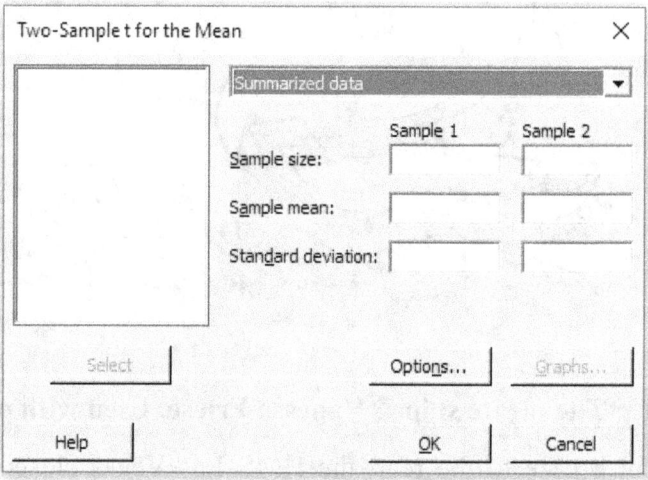

Figure 8.15: Session window for two-sample t for the mean with summarized data

The resulting Minitab session window in Figure 8.16 shows a p value of 0.000; this means they can reject the null hypotheses of "no difference."

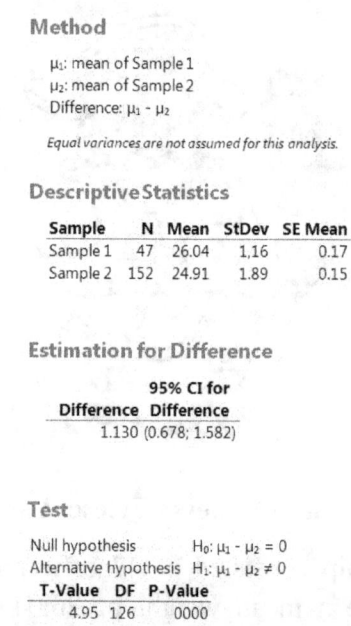

Figure 8.16: Minitab session window for a two-sample t-test

Upon closing closer, grappling hooks were thrown and the boarding action began. The intrepid and inexperienced buccaneers began the arduous climb into the rigging of their prey. "Papa." said Leander. "Yes, Leander?" replied Leander's Papa. "Why does that raccoon have a bazooka?"

"It's probably just an old family heirloom. No worries," responded the old pirate as they climbed higher into the rigging. The old pirate pointed his flintlock at the bazooka carrying raccoon just prior to realizing his flintlock was in the other hand and he was pointing a cutlass at a bazooka-carrying raccoon. "Oops." As the old pirate fumbled while trying not to fall out of the rigging as he switched his weapons between hands, Leander said "Papa." Yes, Leander?" replied Leander's Papa. "Why are there so many cannons behind the gunwale?"

"They can't have a full load of cargo and that many guns or the ship would be too heavy. No worries," responded the old pirate as he realized the ship did indeed have so many guns, therefore it could not be so loaded with cargo, which in turn means the ship was not a cargo ship. Yet, it looked like merchantman. Upon further contemplation, the pirate realized it was a Q-ship.

"Leander" said Leander's Papa. "Yes, Papa?" replied Leander. "We need to go now. I left the coffee machine on at home," said the pirate quietly prior top jumping to the deck of his ship.

"Leander! Get to the helm and put us on a course to the south!" yelled the pirate as he fumbled a cannon into position. Leander stayed calm, took out his compass to find South, and then turned the helm as his Papa traded fire with the Q-ship.

They had set out to impress The Dread Pirate King with a triumphant return, loaded down with plunder. Now, they raced to come under the protective guns of the shore battery on Pirate Island. The vessel was hammered by the raccoon's guns.

Figure 8.17: The Dread Pirate King © Vanessa Friese. Used with permission

The ship's wings were shot off and a fire raged in the rope locker. Yet, the HMS Las Vegas II still sailed onward towards safety. The valiant rogues of the sea tried to give as they got and were not entirely without successes. A cannonball fired by the pirate vessel knocked over a plate of cookies on the Q-ship. Granted, the cannonball continued on and splashed down in the water on the far side of the pursuers. Still, one takes what victories one can in life.

Victories in life can be few and far between; unlike the disguised warship's cannonballs, which were raining down on our bandits like, well, rain.

The pirates were outnumbered by the 47 officers and 152 enlisted. The mean weight of the officers was different than the mean weight of the 152 enlisted. But was there a statistically significant difference in the standard deviations? This could be determined by opening Minitab and going to Stat > Basic Statistics > 2 variances and changing the dropdown to "Sample standard deviations" as shown in Figure 8.18. The sample sizes and standard deviations are then entered into Minitab.

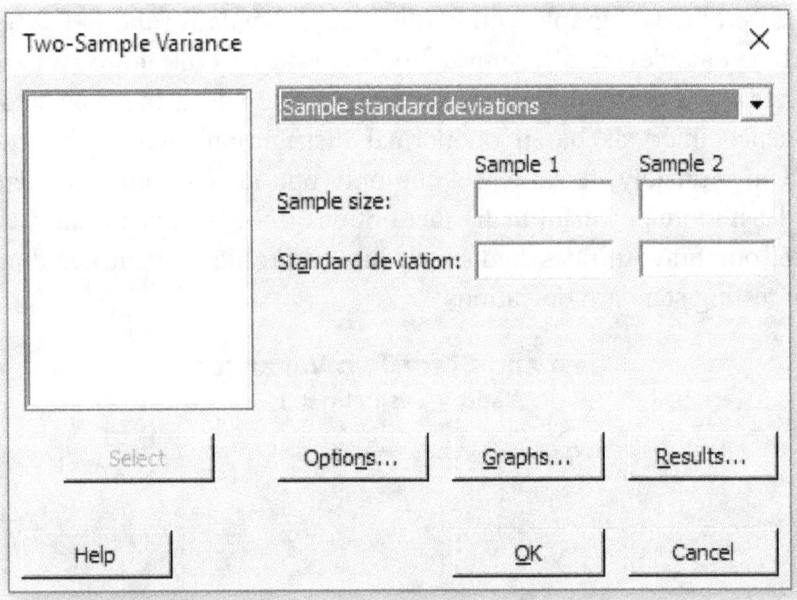

Figure 8.18: Two-Sample Variance screen

The session window shown in Figure 8.19 shows a p value of 0.000 so the null hypotheses can be rejected.

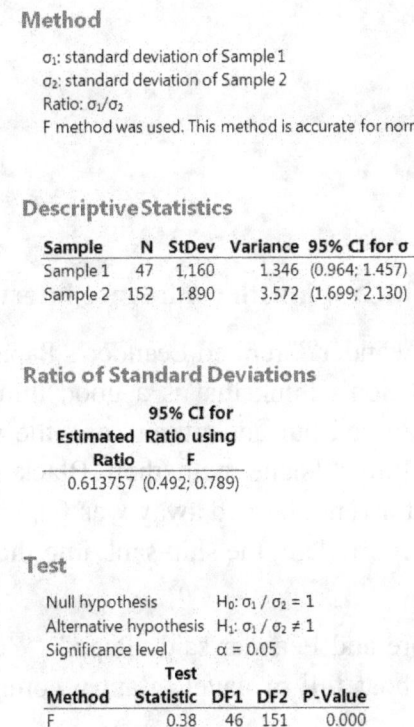

Figure 8.19: Session window for a Two-Variance test

Minitab also provides a graph with confidence intervals for the F-Test (see Figure 8.20). Had the data deviated for normality, the F-test would not be reliable and the pirates would have needed to select "Options." The check mark next to "Use test and confidence intervals based on normal distribution" would then need to be removed. Unfortunately, the F-test is the only option if summarized data is used, but it is at least more powerful than other options if the data is normally distributed. Meanwhile, our brave pirates had much bigger problems than deciding between options for testing standard deviations.

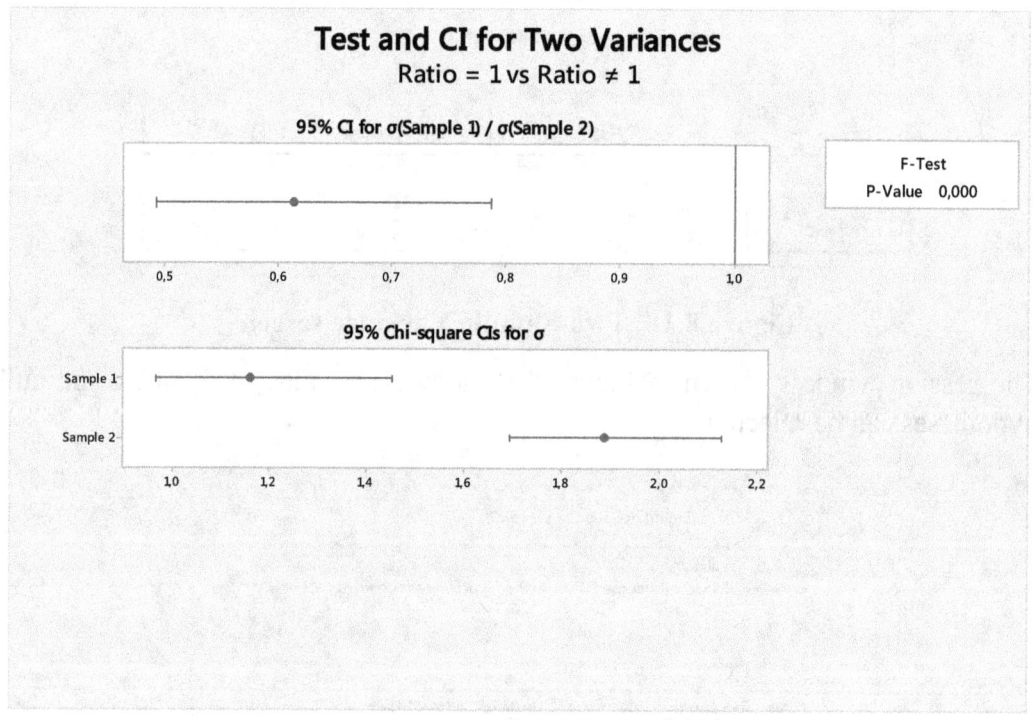

Figure 8.20: Graph with confidence intervals

"Papa." said Leander. "Yes, Leander?" replied Leander's Papa. "Should there be so much water in our ship?" "I don't think that is a good thing," replied the older pirate. Fortunately, fortune favored our adventurers and the warship broke off its pursuit as they approached Pirate Island with their Black Flag flapping in the breeze. Well, the half if it that had not burned away was flapping in the breeze. The fire itself was soon no longer a problem; the ship sank into the mud as they entered a lagoon.

The two pirates trudged ashore and Leander said "Papa." "Yes, Leander?" replied Leander's Papa. "Is that rowboat full of navel infantry coming from the warship going to be a problem?"

"No. Not at all" said the old pirate as he decided it was a good time to go jogging. Ideally, straight into the jungle. They ran and ran and the raccoons stayed on them like a hound dog following a raccoon. Which is rather ironic if you think about it.

After much running, by both the scoundrels of the sea and raccoons, the freebooter's came upon two people at the side of a freshwater stream. "Leander," said Leander's Papa. "Yes, Papa?" replied Leander. "I think those are sea sirens. We should turn and face our pursuers. We'll have a better chance," said the father. "No, they're not. No, we should not. And we won't," said Leander. "It's just an old witch and young witch."

Figure 8.21: Two witches © Vanessa Friese. Used with permission

"Who are you and what are you doing here?" inquired Leander? "We are witches" said the smaller of the two. "We're collecting magic stones."

"Magic stones?" asked Leander?" "Yes" replied the witch to which Leander asked "Do you have an invisibility stone that we could borrow for a moment?"

Seconds later the raccoons dashed out of the jungle with both the buttons on their uniforms and their muskets gleaming in the sun. "I'm looking for two dastardly fellows!" bellowed the captain of naval infantry. The witch both truthfully and honestly answered "I don't see any dastardly fellows around here."

The raccoons then took the witches prisoner while smoke from the remains of the HMS Las Vegas II rose above the jungle. The pirate ship lay in ruins, much like the two sea rogue's dreams of impressing The Dread Pirate King.

"Leander" said Leander's Papa. "Yes, Papa?" replied Leander. "Perhaps we should try cattle rustling."

Figure 8.22: New career

8.32 If you Don't Understand your Statistics, they can Become a Liability

The science writer Michael Shermer, has previously written about something he calls "Darwin's dictum." It's based on a letter Charles Darwin sent to his friend Henry Fawcett in which he stated "How odd it is that anyone should not see that all observation must be for or against some view if it is to be of any service!" Shermer applies this to science (2001), but it applies equally well to statistics, hence I propose a "statistics dictum:" all statistics must be for or against some view to be of any service and the underlying statistical concepts must be understood.

Somebody recently said to me, "I am surprised that you are interested in statistics. I did not expect you to like math." Actually, I found math classes to be pure drudgery. What is there to like about being forced to memorize formulas simply to get a good grade? I have nothing against pure math - only something against teaching math as a rote memorization activity. Statistics, like math, can be taught as merely a collection of formulas one must memorize under penalty of a failing grade, or it can be taught as useful formulas one must understand to accomplish things.

A consultant once told me "Don't bother learning statistics, there are programs that can do it for you." That sounded to me like "Don't bother learning how to write, there are programs that can do that for you." I would not expect an illiterate person to type a letter and I would not want a statistically illiterate person to analyze my data, even if a program does it for them.

A different consultant assisted in the investigation of a failed manufactured product and he was convinced he had identified the root cause because he found a statistically significant difference in a set of measurement data. Unfortunately, the data was from factors that had absolutely no relevance to the problem under investigation. It does not matter if the difference is statistically significant, the area measured could have been removed from the components and this would not have made a difference to the issue under consideration.

Statistics must be used for drawing a conclusion to be of any use. George Box reminds us that "Statistics is, or should be, about scientific investigation and how to do it better, but many statisticians believe it is a branch of mathematics" (1990 p.251). I believe statistics is a tool that engineers should apply to understand data, but many engineers think it has something to do with mats.

An engineer investigating changes in a manufacturing process does not perform a statistical analysis merely to determine if the mean yield of process one is greater than the mean yield of process two with $p < 0.05$. The objective is to determine if there is a difference in the mean yields so that actions can be taken.

Many, if not most, engineering and business degrees require at least one course on statistics and anybody certified as an ASQ Certified Quality Engineer or Six Sigma Black Belt must have some knowledge of statistics. Knowledge of statistics alone will not accomplish anything, only the proper application of statistics with the intent to understand the data will accomplish anything.

In today's industry, statistics are easily assessable to engineers and managers due to the rise in easy to use statistical software packages. This does not mean just anybody can open a statistical software program and crunch numbers, an understanding of statistics is still needed. Conclusions reached through statistical test when the test's assumptions have been violated are worse than no data at all. Changing a manufacturing process due to the results of a Student's t test when the data did not represent the population or a Z test when the population was not normal could mean a large investment in a machine that lowers quality.

Successful professionals in industry can apply the "statistics dictum" by using statistical thinking, which is a "philosophy of learning" consisting of understanding that "All work occurs in a system of interconnected processes," "Variation exists in all processes," and "Understanding and reducing variation are keys to success" (Hoerl and Snee 1995 p.3).

To apply statistical thinking, engineers, technicians and managers must understand the statistical tests they use, as well as the assumptions and limitations of these tests. This requires more than just memorizing the formulas behind the tests. It requires an understanding and an appreciation for statistics. With statistical thinking, statistics can be for or against a view and therefore of service to us. Statistics may for example be of the view that the new process, under the given test conditions, is better than the old process with a specific degree of certainty.

This is not to say that there is no room for studying statistics merely to work with statistics. New statistical methods must be developed and new applications for statistics should be identified. However, even new methods and uses must be for or against some view when they are applied in the real world, or they would serve no purpose.

Statistics is not just a field for statisticians. Engineers and managers in industry must be able to understand and correctly apply statistical concepts as well as evaluate and interpret statistical data. Statistics is too important a topic to be left only to the experts.

Appendix A:

Build a DIY Catapult for Design of Experiments

I needed to find a way to perform experiments to practice using Design of Experiments (DOE), so I built a simple do-it-yourself (DIY) catapult. The basic plan for the catapult is based on the table-top troll catapult, which is available from Will Kalif's Storm the Castle at http://www.stormthecastle.com/catapult/catapult-assembly1.htm.

My catapult is not as attractive as the troll catapult; my goal was to build a catapult with multiple adjustable factors—and not to lay siege to a castle—so I don't mind the rough appearance of my catapult.

The frame consists of two pieces of 40 cm x 4 cm x 2 cm wood, two pieces of 24 cm x 4 cm x 2 cm wood, and eight pieces of 20 cm x 4 cm x 2 cm wood. I could have used other dimensions. The shorter pieces are 50% the length of the long pieces; however, if you use other dimensions, be sure that the wood is thick enough to avoid breaking under the stress of a launch. The catapult arm is made of a 45 cm x 2 cm x 2 cm piece of wood. I could have used a thicker piece for the catapult arm, but wanted something light. Also needed are 16 wood screws. The four screws used to hold the supports to the base must be flathead so the catapult's wooden bottom can sit flat.

I used eighteen small screw eyes to add adjustability and four screw hooks to attach the rubber bands that power the catapult arm. The rubber bands are heavy rubber bands intended for model building, although regular rubber bands could work with a smaller catapult. I used 60 mm diameter, 100 mm diameter and 130 mm diameter rubber bands. The catapult cup can be an actual small cup; I used the bottom of a small plastic bottle.

For projectiles, I could have used small balls—but I wanted a projectile that would not roll or slide much after landing, so I used three small bags of rice as the projectiles. I also used a metal rod cut into pieces for the pivot point on the catapult arm and for the rubber band guides, arm stoppers and arm starting points.

The dimensions can be modified as needed. For example, two pieces of 1" x 2" x 15.75" wood, two pieces of 1" x 2" x 9.5" wood, eight pieces of 1" x 2" x 8" and one piece of 1" x 2" x 18" wood could be used to build the catapult using standard sizes. The catapult can also be scaled-up or scaled-down; just be sure it is wide enough so that it will not tip over.

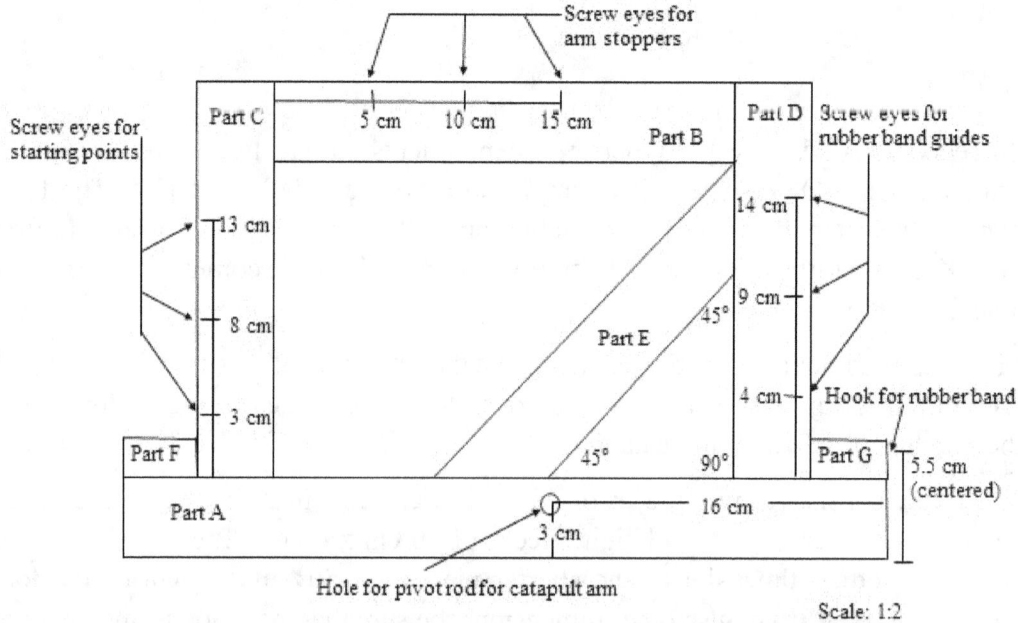

Figure A1: Right-side view of the catapult, without the catapult arm

IMPROVING PRODUCTS, SERVICES AND PROCESSES

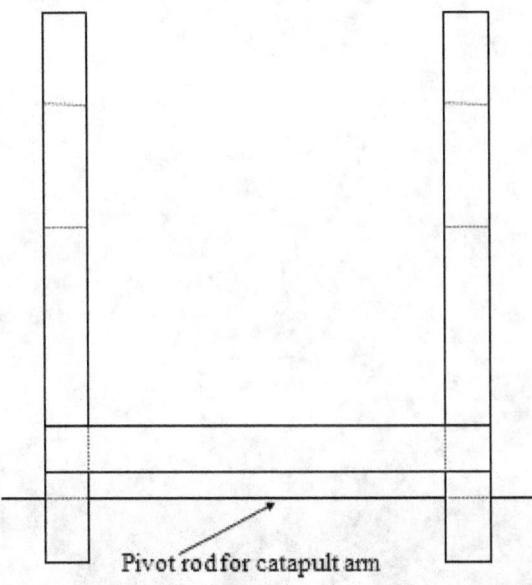

Scale: 1:2

Figure A2: View from the front, again without the catapult arm

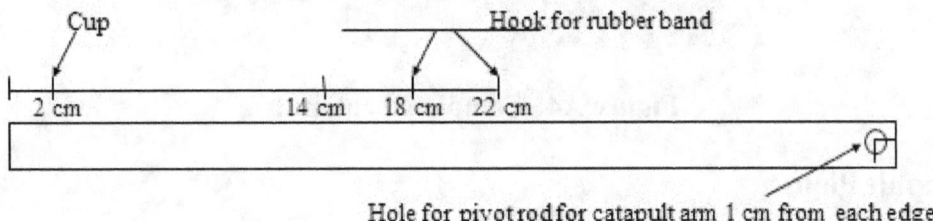

Scale: 1:2

Figure A3: Right-side view of the catapult arm

Figure A4: Completed catapult

Catapult Plans
Part list:

2 Pieces of wood: 40 cm x 4 cm x 2 cm

2 Pieces of wood: 24 cm x 4 cm x 2 cm

8 Pieces of wood: 20 cm x 4 cm x 2 cm

1 Piece of wood: 45 cm x 2 cm x 2 cm

18 eye screws

4 screw hooks

16 Flathead wood screws: 5.0 mm x 60 mm

1 Rubber band: 60 mm diameter

1 Rubber band: 100 mm diameter

1 Rubber band: 130 mm diameter

1 plastic cup: small

1 bag of rice: 25 g

1 bag of rice: 37.5 g

1 bag of rice: 50 g

4 metal rods: 3 mm diameter by 25 cm long

Assembly

Step 1: Cut two pieces of wood to 40 cm x 4 cm x 2 cm to use as the base (part A).

Step 2: Cut two pieces of wood to 24 cm x 4 cm x 2 cm (part B) to connect the supports (parts C and D).

Step 3: Cut eight pieces of wood to 20 cm x 4 cm x 2 cm. The supports (parts C and D) will require 4 pieces; the reinforcement for the supports (part E) will require two pieces and the connectors (parts F and G) will use two pieces.

Step 4: Take two of the 20 cm x 4 cm x 2 cm pieces and cut a 45° angle on each end to fit the support reinforcements (part 4) to the supports (Parts C and D) and base (Part A).

Step 5: Attach the connectors (parts F and G) to the base (part A) using wood screws. NOTE: Predrill the screw holes and countersink if necessary.

Step 6: Attach the supports (parts C and D) to the base (part A) using wood screws.

Step 7: Attach the support reinforcement (part E) to the support (part D) and the base (part A) using wood screws.

Step 8: Attach the support connector (part B) to the supports (parts C and D) using wood screws.

Step 9: Assemble the opposite side by repeating steps 5 through 8 for the opposite side.

Step 10: Drill a hole on each side of the base (part A) for the pivot arm rod. The holes should be slightly larger than the 3 mm metal rod.

Step 11: Drill a hole in the catapult arm for the metal rod.

Step 12: Attach hook for rubber band, screw eyes for rubber band guides, hook screws for arm stoppers and hook screws for starting points to the frame.

Step 13: Attach the hooks for the rubber bands to the catapult arm.

Step 14: Attach the cup to the catapult arm using a wood screw.

Step 15: Attach the catapults arm to the catapult body by first inserting the metal rod into the hole in the base and then pushing it through the hole in the catapult arm. Then push the metal rod all the way through till it comes out of the base on the opposite side. Bend the metal rod on both ends to ensure that it does not fall out of the catapult.

Step 16: Bend the remaining three metal rods into an L shape to use for setting the catapult levels.

Appendix B:

Build a Paper Helicopter for Design of Experiments

A Paper helicopter is often used for DoE training as it provides a response variable (flight time) and many easily changeable factors (leg length, leg width, rotor length, rotor width, paperclip on or off, and paper type). The same helicopter can be used for generating data for other types of statistical methods such as two sample t-tests of the means of the flight times of repeated runs of two different types of helicopters.

Assembly Instructions

Step 1: Cut the paper to a width of 5cm.

Step 2: Cut the paper the length of paper rotor length plus leg length, and add 2 cm for the body.

Step 3: Cut dotted lines at Leg A and Leg C. The length of each cut is 5 cm minus leg width divided by 2.

Step 4: Fold leg A onto leg B.

Step 5: Fold leg C onto leg B.

Step 6: Fold rotor A and rotor B in opposite directions. They should form 90° to the body and be 180° away from each other.

Step 7: For the paper clip version: Add a paper clip to the bottom of the leg

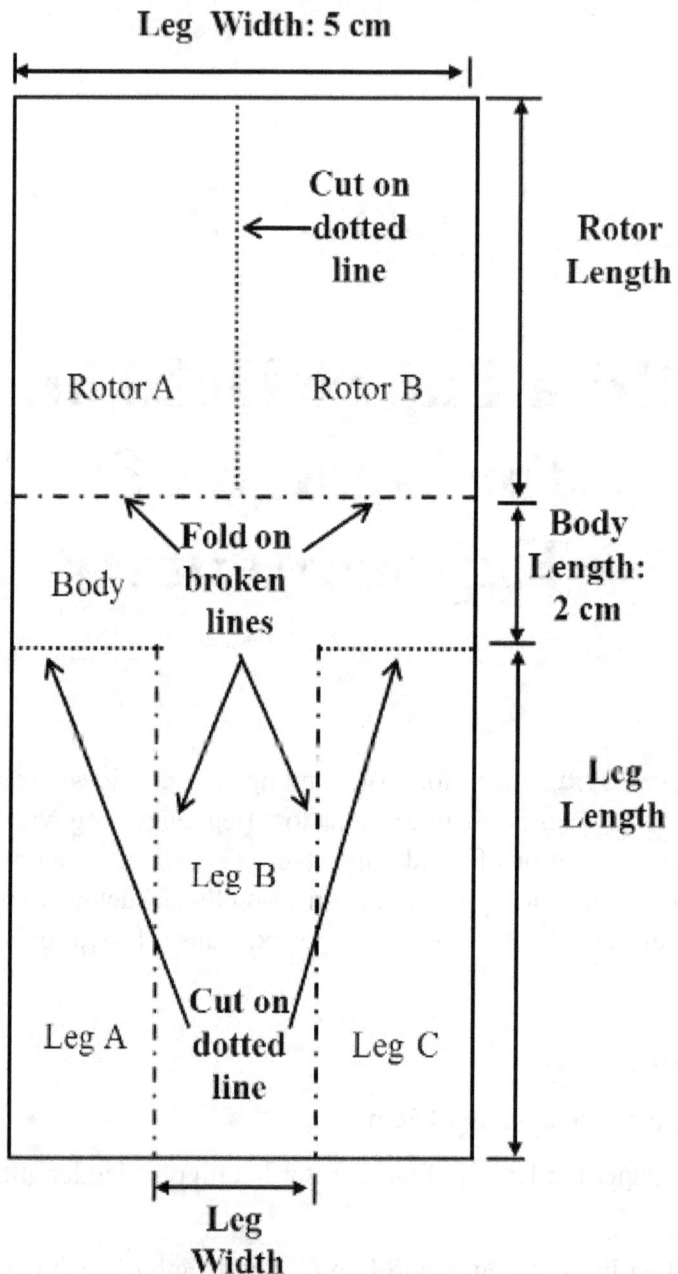

Figure B1: The helicopter plan

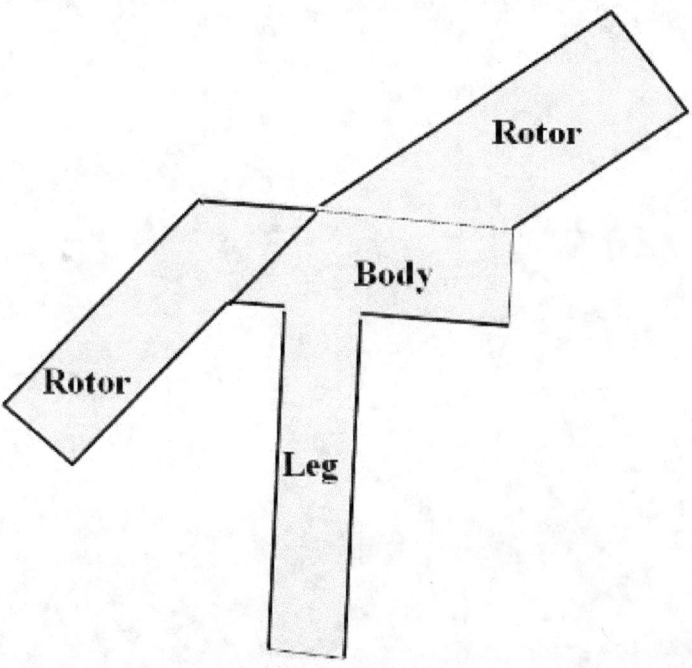

Figure 2: The finished helicopter

Appendix C:

Generating Random Data in Minitab

You can use Minitab's random distribution generate to create data sets for practicing the various statistical methods in Minitab. Go to **Calc > Random Data > Normal** and enter the number or row to generate, the name of the column to store the data in, the mean, and the standard deviation. You can either select a column to store the data in or enter a name; however, spaces are viewed as a separate column name so the words must run together if you want a name consisting of more than one word. The same can be done for other types of distributions. Tables A3.1 to A3.7 contain examples that can be used as practice exercises.

Distribution	Normal	Normal
Number of rows	22	24
Column label	DiameterA	DiameterB
Mean	12.3	12.28
Standard deviation	0.2	0.17
Distribution	Normal	Normal
Task: Compare using individual value plots and boxplots. Then compare the means using a 2-sample t-test		

Table A3.1: First graphs and 2-sample t-test exorcise

Distribution	Normal	Normal
Number of rows	30	30
Column label	WeightA	Weight2
Mean	12.3	12.28
Standard deviation	0.2	0.17
Distribution	Normal	Normal
Task: Compare using individual value plots and boxplots. Then compare the means using a 2-sample t-test			

Table A3.2: Second graphs and 2-sample t-test exercise

Distribution	Normal	Normal	Normal	Normal
Number of rows	25	25	25	25
Column label	LengthA	LengthB	LengthC	LengthD
Mean	48.4	48	47.8	48.3
Standard deviation	0.9	0.7	0.8	0.9
Task: Perform a One-Way ANOVA				

Table A3.3: ANOVA exercise

Distribution	Exponential
Number of rows	30
Column label	WeightA
Scale	1
Threshold	5
Task: Asses normality using a probability plot	

Table A3.4: Probability plot exercise with non-normally distributed data

Distribution	Normal
Number of rows	30
Column label	WeightB
Mean	78
Standard deviation	2
Task: Asses normality using a probability plot	

Table A3.5: Probability plot exercise with normally distributed data

Distribution	Normal
Number of rows	150
Column label	Supplier A
Mean	14
Standard deviation	0.2
Task: Create an I-MR chart; then create an Xbar-R chart with subgroup size 5	

Table A3.6: Control chart exercise

Distribution	Normal
Number of rows	100
Column label	Supplier B
Mean	22.1
Standard deviation	0.4
Task: Asses the capability using a subgroup size of one and a specification of 22.0 +/-1.5	

Table A3.7: Capability exercise

References

Atwood, Horace. 1925. *The Standard Deviation in the Weight of White Leghorn Eggs*. Morgantown, WV: Agricultural Experiment Station.

Barsalou, Matthew A. 2015. *Statistics for Six Sigma Black Belts*. Milwaukee. WI: Quality Press.

Benbow, Donald W. and T.M. Kubiak. 2009. *The Certified Six Sigma Black Belt Handbook*. Milwaukee. WI: Quality Press.

Borror, Connie. M. (ed.) 2009. *The Certified Quality Engineer Handbook* (3rd ed.). Milwaukee. WI: Quality Press.

Box, George .E.P. and K.B. Wilson. 1951. "On the Experimental Attainment of Optimum Conditions." *Journal of the Royal Statistical Society. Series B. Statistical Methodology* 13: 1-45.

Box George E.P. 1976. "Science and Statistics." *Journal of the American Statistical Association*. 71, no. 356: 791-799.

Box, George E.P. 1990. "Commentary on Communications Between Statisticians and Engineers/Physical Scientists." *Technometrics* 32, no. 3: 251-252.

Box, George E.P. 1992. "Teaching Engineers Experimental Design with a Paper Helicopter." *Quality Engineering* 4, no. 3: 453-459.

Box, George E.P., J. Stuart Hunter, and William G. Hunter. 2005. *Statistics for Experimenters: Design, Innovation, and Discovery* (2nd ed.). Hoboken, NJ: John Wiley & Sons.

Breyfogle, Forrest III. 2003.*Implementing Six Sigma: Smarter Solutions® using Statistical Methods*. (2nd). Hoboken, NJ: John Wiley & Sons.

Breyfogle, Forrest III. 2008. *Integrated Enterprise Excellence Volume III - Improvement Project Execution: A Management and Black Belt Guide for Going Beyond Lean Six Sigma and the Balanced Scorecard*. Citius Publishing, Inc.

Coca-Cola Company. 2012. "The Real Story of new Coke." Accessed 26 Aug. 2017 from http://www.coca-colacompany.com/stories/coke-lore-new-coke.

Deming, W. Edwards. 1989. *Out of the Crisis*. Cambridge, MA: Massachusetts Institute of Technology.

Dhar, Michael. 2013. "Surviving a Zombie Apocalypse: Just do the Math." *Live Science*. https://www.livescience.com/38527-surviving-a-zombie-apocalypse-math.html. Accessed 26 Aug. 2017.

Dr. Seuss, Jack Prelutsky, and Lane Smith. 1998. *Hooray for Diffendoofer Day*. New York, NY: Random House.

Durivage, Mark Allen. 2015. *Practical Engineering, Process, and Reliability Statistics*. Milwaukee. WI: Quality Press.

Durivage, Mark Allen. 2016. *Practical Design of Experiments: A Guide for Optimizing Designs and Processes*. Milwaukee. WI: Quality Press.

Filippone, Peggy Trowbridge. 2017. "Turkey Cooking Times: Know How Long to Roast That Bird." *The Spruce*. Accessed 26 Aug. 2017 from https://www.thespruce.com/turkey-cooking-times-1807695.

Franz Joseph Designs. 1975. *Star Trek Blueprints*. New York, NY: Ballantine Books Inc.

Freedman, David, Robert Pisani, and Roger Purves. 1978. *Statistics*. New York, NY: W.W. Norton & Company.

Fisher, Ronald A. 1971. *The Design of Experiments*. New York, NY: Hafner Publishing Company.

Frost, Jim. 2012. "How to Be a Ghost Hunter with a Statistical Mindset." *The Minitab Blog*. Accessed 26 Aug. 2017 from http://blog.minitab.com/blog/adventures-in-statistics-2/how-to-be-a-ghost-hunter-with-a-statistical-mindset.

Smith, E.E. 1966b. *The Skylark of Space*. New York, NY: Pyramid Books.

Smith, Joel. 2015. "Poisson Processes and Probability of Poop." *The Minitab Blog*. Accessed 26 Aug. 2017 from http://blog.minitab.com/blog/fun-with-statistics/poisson-processes-and-probability-of-poop.

Startreck.com. 2017. Accessed 26 Aug. 2017 from http://www.startrek.com/.

Stephens, Larry J. 2004. *Advanced Statistics Demystified: A Self-Teaching Guide*. New York, NY: McGraw Hill.

Student. 1908. "The Probable Error of a Mean." *Biometrika* 6, no: 1: 1-25.

Tukey, John. W. 1977. *Exploratory Data Analysis*. Reading, MA: Addison-Wesley.

Turner, Tina. 1985. "Mad Max Beyond Thunderdome- Original Motion Picture Soundtrack." *Capital Records*. SWAV-12429. LP Album.

VanDerWerff, Todd. 2015. "The Violent, Beautiful World of the Must-See New Movie Mad Max: Fury Road, Explained." *Vox*. Accessed 26 Aug. 2017 from https://www.vox.com/2015/5/15/8612481/mad-max-review-fury-road.

Vining, Geoffrey and Scott M. Kowalski. 2006. *Statistical Methods for Engineers*. (2nd ed.). Belmont, CA: Thompson Higher Education.

Weimer, Richard C. 1993. *Statistics* (2nd ed.). Dubuque, IA: Wm. C. Brown Publishers.

Wheeler, Donald J. 1995. *Advanced Topics in Statistical Process Control: The Power of Shewhart's Charts*. Knoxville, TN: SPC Press.

Wheeler, Donald J. 2009. *Twenty Things you Need to Know*. Knoxville, TN: SPC Press.

Witte, Robert S: 1993. 1993. *Statistics*. (4th ed.). Harcourt Brace College Publishers.XKCD. 2017. Significant. Accessed 26 Aug. 2017 from https://xkcd.com/882/.

Ziliak, Stephen T., Deidre N. McCloskey. 2012. *The Cult of Statistical Significance; How the Standard Error Costs us Jobs, Justice, and Lives*. New York, NY: The University of Michigan Press, Ann Arbor, MI.

www.ingramcontent.com/pod-product-compliance
Lightning Source LLC
Chambersburg PA
CBHW080543220526
45466CB00010B/3018